C000179246

Cheerfulness

Garrison Keillor

also by Garrison Keillor

Serenity at 70, Gaiety at 80, 2022
Boom Town, 2022
That Time of Year: A Minnesota Life, 2020
The Lake Wobegon Virus, 2020
Living with Limericks, 2019
The Keillor Reader, 2014
O, What a Luxury, 2013
Guy Noir and the Straight Skinny, 2012
A Christmas Blizzard, 2009
Pilgrims, 2009
Life Among the Lutherans, 2009
77 Love Sonnets, 2009
Liberty, 2008
Pontoon, 2007
Daddy's Girl, 2005
Homegrown Democrat, 2004
Love Me, 2003
In Search of Lake Wobegon, 2001
Lake Wobegon Summer 1956, 2001
ME, 1999
Wobegon Boy, 1997
The Old Man Who Loved Cheese, 1996
The Sandy Bottom Orchestra, 1996
Cat You Better Come Home, 1995
The Book of Guys, 1993
WLT, 1991
We Are Still Married, 1989
Leaving Home, 1988
Lake Wobegon Days, 1985
Happy to Be Here, 1981

Cheerfulness

Garrison Keillor

Prairie Home Productions
Minneapolis, MN

Copyright © 2023 by Garrison Keillor

All rights reserved. Published in the United States by Prairie Home Productions. No part of this book may be reproduced in any manner without the express written consent of the publisher, except in the case of brief excerpts in critical reviews or articles. All inquiries should be addressed to Prairie Home Productions, P.O. Box 2090, Minneapolis, MN 55402.

Visit our website at garrisonkeillor.com

First Edition

Library of Congress Control Number: 2023936999
ISBN: 979-8-9882818-0-1

Cover and book interior design by David Provolo
Cover photo by Mylène Fernandes
Illustration by Charles Keillor

I'd go see my therapist and tell her I was very happy and she'd explain to me why I wasn't, that I was in denial, and that I needed her to clarify my pain and trace it back to childhood trauma, that she couldn't work with me if I insisted on stifling my depression, but fortunately for me she was much older than I and when she died I felt bad of course but only for a few days and then I got this strange feeling of liberation. I had hired the woman to make me feel bad and now it was over and I'm only 47, I have half a lifetime ahead of me, maybe more. And my Tuesdays and Thursdays at 11 a.m. are completely free to do whatever I like with them, to go look at art, or walk in the park, or have lunch with you. So how are you? You look good. How's your hamburger?

A woman friend,
at lunch, last March,
in N.Y.C., on Columbus Avenue

I've written a book about cheer
As a light at the end of a pier
To assist navigation
And find this way station
And not be out there but in here.
This isn't a school to attend
And learn to attain and ascend,
It's a place to moor
And know that you're
Sure of your bearings, my friend.
Amidst crosscurrents, winds blowing,
Come into port and stop rowing,
Put trouble behind,
Be of good mind,
Good humor, good cheer,
Good cheer is contagious,
Can make you courageous
To set sail and head where you're going.

1

Cheerfulness

It's a great American virtue, the essence of who we are when we're cooking with gas: enthusiasm, high spirits, rise and shine, qwitcher bellyaching, wake up and die right, pick up your feet, step up to the plate and swing for the fences. Smile, dammit. Dance like you mean it and give it some pizzazz, clap on the backbeat. Do your best and forget the rest, da doo ron ron ron da doo ron ron. Praise the Lord and pass the ammunition, hang by your thumbs and write when you get work, whoopitiyiyo git along little cowboys—and I am an American, I don't eat my cheeseburger in a croissant, don't look for a church that serves a French wine and a sourdough wafer for Communion, don't use words like *dodgy, bonkers, knack-ered, or chuffed*. When my team scores, I don't shout, *Très bien!!* I don't indulge in dread and dismay. Yes, I can make a list of evils and perils and injustices in the world, but I believe in a positive attitude and I know that one can do only so much and one should do that much and do it cheerfully. Dread is communicable: healthy rats fed fecal matter from depressed humans demonstrated depressive behavior, including anhedonia and anxiety—crap is bad for the brain. Nothing good comes from this. Despair is surrender. Put your shoulder to the wheel. And wash your hands.

We live in an Age of Gloom, or so I read, and some people blame electronics, but I love my cellphone and laptop, and others blame the decline of Protestantism, but I grew up fundamentalist so I don't, and others blame bad food. Too much grease and when there's a potluck supper, busy people tend to stop at Walmart or a SuperAmerica station and pick up a potato salad that was manufactured a month ago and shipped in tanker trucks and it's depressing compared to Grandma's, which she devoted an hour to making fresh from chopped celery, chives, green onions, homemade mayonnaise, mustard, dill, and paprika. You ate it and knew that Grandma cared about you. The great potato salad creators are passing from the scene, replaced by numbskulls so busy online they're willing to bring garbage to the communal table.

I take no position on that, since I like a Big Mac as well as anybody and I've bought food in plastic containers from refrigerated units at gas stations and never looked at the expiration date. And I am a cheerful man.

I rise early, make coffee, look out at the rooftops and I feel lucky. Today is my day. Other people, God bless them, go see their therapist. I never did. What would we talk about? I enjoy my work, I love my wife, my heart got repaired years ago so I didn't die at 59 when I was supposed to. My dream life is mostly very chipper, sociable, sometimes I'm hauling crates of fish along a wharf in the Orkney Islands, one Orker bursts into song and we all sing together, me singing bass in a language I don't understand, and I'm rather contented in my sleep. Why should I argue with gifts? A therapist would turn this inside out and make it a form of denial. It isn't. I'd tell her the joke about the man walking by the insane asylum, hearing the lunatics yelling, "Twenty-one! Twenty-one!" and he puts his eye to a hole in the fence to see what's going on and they poke him in the eye and yell, "Twenty-two! Twenty-two!" and she'd find a hidden meaning in it but there isn't one, just a sharp stick. I'm not going to talk about my father because he's dead and one does not speak ill of the dead, they are waiting for us and we will join them soon enough, meanwhile I feel good and thank you very much for asking. Sometimes, in church, when peace, like a river, attendeth my way, I feel actually joyful, I truly do.

I used to be cool and ironic and monosyllabic and now I'm a garrulous old man who's about to lecture you about the importance of good manners (YAWN) and cheerfulness especially in grim situations such as 6 a.m. on a dark February morning standing in an endless line waiting to go through airport security and a TSA sniffer dog is walking along the line giving it a prison-camp feel and sleepy people toting baggage are waiting and the old man recalls pre-terrorist days when you walked straight to your gate, no questions asked, and he feels—well— *sort of abused.* And then a teenage girl walks past the checker's booth to the end of the conveyor belt to put her stuff in the plastic bins and her lurching gait indicates some sort of brain injury. She seems to be alone. She also seems quite proud of managing in this situation, emptying her pockets, adopting the correct stance in the scanner, stepping out to be patted down by a TSA lady who then puts an arm around her and says something and the girl grins.

It's a beautiful little moment of kindness. The cheerfulness of this kid making her way in the world. It reminds me of my friend Earl, who is 80 like me, who visits his wife every day at her care center and takes her for a walk, which cheers her up despite her dementia; he keeps in touch with his daughter who struggles with diabetes and an alcoholic husband; Earl is an old Democrat who is critical of the cluelessness of the progressive left when it comes to managing city government and law enforcement; but despite all this, he is very good company on the phone, never complains, savors the goodness of life.

I talked to Earl the night before the 6 a.m. line at Security and I think of him as I watch the girl collecting her stuff at the end of the conveyor. She feels good about herself and this strikes me as heroic.

So when I hear a woman behind me say, "This is the last time I fly early in the morning. This is just unbearable" (except she put another word ahead of "unbearable"), I turned and said, "Did you hear about the guy who was afraid of bears in the woods." She shook her head. "His friend told him that if a bear chases you, just run fast, and if the bear gets close, just reach back and grab a handful and throw it at him. The guy says, "A handful of what?" "Oh, don't worry, it'll be there. It'll be there."

"Oh for God's sake," she said, and then she laughed. She said, "I can't believe you told me that joke." I said that I couldn't believe it either. She said she was going to Milwaukee to see her brother and she intended to tell him that joke. So we got into a little conversation about Milwaukee. She said, "Have a nice day," and I said, "I'm having it."

It was not always sunshine and roses with me. I grew up in a small fundamentalist cult where the singing sounded like a fishing village mourning for the sailors lost in the storm. I spent years in a sad marriage eating meals in silence and wrote stricken verse and long anguished letters, had a couple brain seizures that made me contemplate becoming a vegetable, perhaps a potato, but recovered and finally realized that anguish is for younger people and now was the time to pull up my socks, so one day, having exhausted the possibilities of tobacco after twenty years, I quit a three-pack-a-day chain-smoking habit simply by not smoking (duh)—a simple course correction, the lady in the dashboard saying, "When possible, make a legal U-turn," and I did and that turned me into a certified optimist. Smoking was an affectation turned addictive. I stopped it. A powerful deadly habit thrown overboard. I thought, "You have a good life and be grateful for it and no more mewling and sniveling." I have mostly stuck to that rule.

Life is good. Coffee has taken great strides forward. There are more fragrances of soap than ever before. Rosemary, basil, tarragon, coriander: formerly on your spice shelf, now in the shower stall. I bought pumpkin-seed/flax granola recently, something I never knew existed. Can rhubarb/radish/garbanzo granola be far behind? The slots in your toaster are wider to accommodate thick slices of baguette. Music has become a disposable commodity like toilet paper: the 45 and the CD are gone, replaced by streaming, which requires no investment. Your phone used to be on a short leash and the whole family could hear your conversation and now you can walk away from home and exchange intimate confidences if you have any. The phone is my friend. I press the Map app and a blinking blue dot shows me where I am, and I can type "mailbox" into the Search bar and it shows me where the corner mailbox is, 200 feet away. I already knew that but it's good to have it confirmed. The language has expanded: LOL, FOMO, emo, genome, OMG, gender identity, selfie, virtual reality, sus, fam, tweet, top loading, canceled, indigeneity, witchu, wonk, woke, damfino. I come from the era of Larry and Gary and now you have boys named Aidan and Liam, Conor, Cathal, Dylan, Minnesota kids enjoying the luxury of being Celtic. Girls with the names of goddesses and divas, Arabella, Aurora, Artemis, Ophelia, Anastasia. We have the Dairy Queen Butterfinger Blizzard if you live near a Dairy Queen. Unscrewable bottle caps—no need to search for a bottle opener (once known as the "church key," and no more). Shampoo and conditioner combined in one container. The list goes on and on. We have Alexa who when I say, "Alexa, play the Rolling Stones' 'Brown Sugar,'" she does it. I can get the Stones on YouTube but then I have to watch a commercial for a retirement home, a laxative, and Viagra. And the tremendous variety of coffee cups! We used to get coffee cups as premiums at the gas station, all the same pastel yellow or green, and now we have cups with humorous sayings on them, Monet landscapes, the insignia of your college, an Emily Dickinson poem, you choose a cup that expresses your true distinctive self. We didn't used to be so distinct.

I am no role model, my children. I have the face of a gravedigger, I get less exercise than a house cat, my water intake is less than that of a lizard, I am a small island of competence in an ocean of ignorance, I have three ex-girlfriends who wouldn't be good character references, and yet I feel darned good, thanks to excellent medical care. I avoided doctors with WASPy names like Postlethwaite or Dimbleby-Pritchett and ones whose secretary put me on Hold and I had to listen to several minutes of flute music. I chose women doctors, knowing that women have to be smarter to get ahead in medicine. And what Jane tells me is that your most crucial health decision is the choice of your parents and I chose two who believed in longevity so I am a cheerful man and walk on the sunny side and meet the world's indifference with a light heart. I put my bare feet on the wood floor at 6 a.m., pull my pants on, left leg first, then the right, not holding onto anything though I'm 80 and a little off-balance and if my right foot gets snagged on fabric it's suddenly like mounting a bucking horse, but I buckle my belt and go forth to live my life. I'm a Minnesotan and have my head on straight so I get to the work I was put here to do. Some lucky nights I am awakened at 3 or 4 by a bright idea and I slip out of bed and put it on paper. When COVID came along, I accepted it as a gift and we isolated ourselves in an apartment on the Upper West Side of Manhattan like Aida locked in a tomb with her lover, Radamès, but with grocery deliveries, and Lulu our housekeeper came on Tuesdays.

A pandemic is a rare opportunity for a writer: I sat in a quiet room, nowhere to go, nothing to do, and I spun two novels, a memoir, and a weekly column. Most of the gifted artists I knew—musicians, actors, comedians—were out of work, whereas I, the writer of homely tropes and truisms, was busier than ever. The audience for a white male author is smaller than the state of Rhode Island but my writing is improving and I'm happy about that. My aunt Eleanor said, "We are all islands in the sea of life and seldom do our peripheries touch," which surely was true during the pandemic but my island and Jenny's often brushed peripheries and that was highly pleasurable and then of course there is the telephone.

I accept that I'm a white male though I don't consider it definitive any more than shoe size is. I'm of Scots-Yorkshire ancestry, people bred to endure cold precipitation. Give us a whole day of hard rain and we feel at home. We are comfortable with silence and when we do speak, we utter short sentences rather than gusts. We aren't prone to weeping though I sometimes do in church when it strikes me that God loves me. And when the woman I love sits on my lap, her head against mine, and says, "I need you," I am moved, deeply. I don't hurl brushfuls of paint at a canvas or compose a crashing sonata or write a long poem, unpunctuated, all lower-case, but I am moved. I knew I needed her but you can't assume it's mutual, so hearing it cheers me up. I don't question her about the specific needs I satisfy, abstract theory is good enough.

Ralph Waldo Emerson, the Sage of Concord, the Champion of Cheerfulness, wrote back in the days of slavery when the beloved country was breaking in two:

Finish every day and be done with it. You have done what you could; some blunders and absurdities no doubt crept in; forget them as soon as you can. Tomorrow is a new day; you shall begin it well and serenely, and with too high a spirit to be cumbered with your old nonsense. Nothing great is achieved without enthusiasm.

For this and much more that he said, Emerson is the true father of his country, not the guy with the powdered hair and the teeth made of ivory and whatnot. All he said was "I cannot tell a lie" and that is simply not true. He was lucky in war, kept his mouth shut because of his bad teeth, and served as president before there was investigative journalism. I'd say he was the great-uncle of his country, maybe the stepfather. When I saw his picture next to Lincoln's on our classroom wall, I thought he was Lincoln's wife and not all that attractive.

When my daughter was 18, I went to prom at her school and stood in the gym with other parents as our kids processed in, boys in suits and ties, girls in prom dresses, the beams overhead and the tile walls all gay and glittery with banners and baubles, and a local rock band of codgers my age struck up "Brown-Eyed Girl" and our kids went wild, laughing and a-running, skipping and a-jumping, just like the song says, and we parents sang, "You, my brown-eyed girl, do you remember when we used to sing, *Sha la la la la la la la la la lah de dah.*" And then "So Fine" (*My baby's so doggone fine, she sends those chills up and down my spine*). Old men with historic Stratocasters playing for our kids songs from my long-ago youth, the lead guitarist almost bald but with a slender gray ponytail like a clothesline coming out of the back of his head, playing his four or five good licks with great delight, and then *My heart went boom when I crossed the room and I held her hand in mine.*

This was a school for kids we once called "handicapped," now we say "learning challenged" or "on the spectrum" but when the music played they were all equal in the eyes of the Lord. I went to public school: you

stood on the corner, you boarded the bus, it took you to
school. This school is one that each of us parents searched
desperately for as our child sank into the academic
slough. Many of the kids in the gym look as ordinary
as you or me, and others are a little off-balance, quirky
movements of head or arms, a speech abnormality. My
heart clutches to see them dancing and I remember how
shitty we were to kids like them when I was their age, it
was so uncool to be seen with them and they never went
to school dances, and here they were, ecstatic, including a girl injured as an infant who's blind in one eye,
walks with a lurch, one arm semi-paralyzed, and she was
dancing like mad, and it struck me that jumping around
on the dance floor these kids don't feel there's anything
wrong with them. They are completely transported. Van
Morrison didn't write "Brown-Eyed Girl" as a therapeu-
tic exercise, but here they are, dancing with abandon,
and Grandpa Guitar is happy too, the wild boogying of
oddballs a vision of paradise, and when the slow Father-
Daughter dance struck up, I took my girl in my arms
and I sang it to her, *I feel happy inside, it's such a feeling
that my love I can't hide, Oooooo.*"

That's my vision of cheerfulness. You get some hard
knocks in life but you still dance and let your heart sing.
I didn't get knocked as hard as those kids did and any
despair I feel is simply grandiosity: get over it.

My girl is a hugger and snuggler like her mother and

when I put my arms around her I feel I'm hugging my aunts, who are all gone, and my mother, though she was a shoulder-patter like me. I never hugged my dad except as a small child. When my girl was three, I took her to visit my dad who lay dying in the house I grew up in, the house he built in a cornfield in Minnesota in 1947, and he was delighted to see her. He moved a foot under the blanket and she reached for it and he moved it away and she grabbed for it and it got away again. She laughed, playing this little game. She was my best gift to him, his last grandchild. He was 88, I was 55. My father who'd been through miserable procedures in ERs and said, "No more" and was waiting to die and he was pleased as could be by the laughter of a little girl. She was delighted by him. And now I'm delighted to see her dancing to the grandpa band at the prom in the gym. God is good and His lovingkindness endures for generations.

I come from cheerful people. John and Grace kept a good humor and loved each other dearly. When Dad went into a luncheonette he always made small talk with the waitress: *Looks like we're finally getting spring. We can use the rain, that's for sure. Boy, that apple pie sure looks good. You wouldn't happen to have some cheese with that, would you? Apple pie without the cheese is like a hug without the squeeze.* The little chirps and murmurs, the sweet drizzle of small talk. He spoke it well. Mother adored comedians, Jack Benny, George Gobel, Lucille Ball. My parents courted during the Depression, married in '37, went through the War, built a house in the country, had six kids whom Dad worked two jobs to support while Mother cooked and cleaned and slaved in the kitchen every August, canning fruit and vegetables from a half-acre garden, the pressure cooker steaming, her hair damp with sweat, and I cannot remember them ever complaining about the unfairness of life or envying the privileged who bought their produce at SuperValu. Sometimes she said *Darn it* or *Oh, for crying out loud.*

Mother did not encourage complaint—"Other people have it worse than you," she said, referring to children in China. She also said, "If you don't have something nice to say, don't say anything at all." Which eliminated journalism as a career.

She admired FDR and Eleanor because they cared about the poor. My dad felt that the WPA was relief for the lazy, We Poke Along. Their difference of opinion never got in the way of their love for each other. Sometimes I'd find her sitting in his lap, the parents of six kissing. He was a little sheepish, she was not. Once I found a sex manual titled *Light On Dark Corners* in their bedroom and though it was dense with euphemisms, I understood that my parents lay naked in bed and did stuff, and I hoped to emulate this someday, whatever it exactly was.

I feel good in the morning, especially since I quit drinking in 2002. (The way to do it is to do it.) I have a clear head and I light a low flame under the skillet and think of the chicken as I crack the two eggs but when I fry the sausage, I don't think of the pig. The egg is a work of art; the sausage is a product. As a young man I wanted to make art but I didn't want to work in the academic factory to support my art, so I chose to do radio, which is a form of sausage. I admire the egg but I enjoy the sausage more. And it makes me feel cheerful, a good thing at the start of day before mistakes accumulate. My life is a series of mistakes. It's cold in Minnesota so I went into radio because it's indoors and vacuum tubes gave off heat. I set out to write humorous fiction à la Thurber and Benchley and S.J. Perelman, who were like the uncles I wished I had. I didn't write serious fiction because that's what I'd been forced to read by teachers and it had a penal quality about it. I made these big decisions based on no information and they turned out well. I've enjoyed lavish freedom to do homespun narratives sponsored by Powdermilk Biscuits and the American Duct Tape Council and talk about the poet Sylvia Plath who was full of sorrow and wrath and the day that she dove headfirst in the stove, she should've just had a warm bath—and if it was a modest enterprise, well, it was my own choice.

I have a dark side. I do not believe in regular exercise;

I believe that an exemplary healthful lifestyle makes it more likely I'd be struck by a marble plinth falling off a facade as I walk to the health club. I can't define "plinth" but I know it would kill me. I am quite cheerful staying home and I get my exercise reaching for things on high shelves.

My Grandma Dora sang me to sleep with "Poor Babes in the Woods," lost in a snowstorm: "they sobbed and they sighed and they bitterly cried, and the poor little things, they lay down and died"—not a song Mister Rogers ever sang. Grandma did not tell us to look the other way when she chopped the head off a chicken. Death was a part of our lives. Not many children today have observed a beloved relative swinging an axe and a headless chicken flapping around on the bloody ground. I have. You must be aware of death to fully appreciate the goodness of life.

I learned cheerfulness from my folks. They had known hard times and now having a home, a garden, a car, gave them pleasure, and they savored it. I grew up in the Fifties, when my shyness led some of my aunts and teachers to imagine I was gifted. Actually I was autistic, not artistic, but autism hadn't been invented yet, so I had the advantage of ignorance and by the time I learned what the problem was, it was too late for remedial ed,

I was in my forties, a published writer with a popular radio show.

I was born with a congenital mitral valve defect that killed off two of my uncles in their late fifties. They simply dropped dead. Had I been born thirty years earlier, I'd be dead too. The defect kept me off the football team, spared me from brain injury, and the hometown paper hired me, at age 14, to write sports and I did my best to make a mediocre team valiant in print, thus my disability opened the door to a career in fiction.

I was lucky to live in Minnesota, a state proud of its numerous colleges and its homebred writers like Sinclair Lewis and Scott Fitzgerald, proud of its work ethic and Lutheran modesty and the call to public service and not so keen about euphoria so there was no reliable criminal element to supply dope, everything we obtained in college was substandard and diluted, the hashish was full of mulch, the cocaine was half talcum powder, the cannabis smelled of Maxwell House, the mushrooms were no more hallucinogenic than Campbell's soup, so I didn't experience euphoria until I was 45 and had two wisdom teeth extracted and was sedated and given painkillers, a dreamy experience. If I'd experienced it when I was 21, it could've sent me spinning into thirty years of rehab. But at 45 you know enough to know that real life is preferable to having a headful of golden mist.

In my twenties, I considered the idea of dying young

and becoming immortal like James Dean in his sports car crash or Buddy Holly in the little plane in the snowstorm or Dylan Thomas drowning in drink, dying on their way up in the world, no sad decline into middle-aged mediocrity. Maybe this morbid thought came from my Scots heritage. Bluegrass comes from Scottish balladry, songs about dying bridegrooms and the bride taking poison at the burial and throwing herself into his grave. That sort of song.

Scotland is where golf comes from, a game that shows us the worst aspects of ourselves, potato-faced men in yellow pants riding electric carts in search of a white ball in tall grass and whacking it into a body of water and cursing God's creation and then sitting in a clubhouse and getting soused on mint juleps and complaining about the income tax.

Thank God, I realized that immortality is no substitute for life itself. I missed an opportunity at early death in 1962 when, on a straight stretch in Isanti County on a two-lane highway, I got my '56 Ford up to 100 mph and a pickup truck suddenly eased out of a driveway up ahead and onto the highway. In a split second, I swerved to go behind him and it was a good choice—he didn't see me and try to back up—otherwise he and I would've been forever joined in a headline. Anyway I'd done nothing worth immortalization, just introspective stuff—"He looked out the window and saw the reflection of his own pale face against the drifted snow. She was gone. Like everyone else."—A few years later I almost died young again when I bought a king-size mattress from a furniture warehouse and tied it to the roof of my car with a piece of twine and it blew off as I drove home on the freeway and I pulled over and ran back to rescue it and a big rig blew past me blasting his horn. A memorable thing, the Doppler effect of a semi horn doing 70 a few feet away. In 1983 my brother Philip and I canoed into a deep cavern in Devil's Island on Lake Superior, attracted by the dancing reflections on the cavern ceiling and paddled way in until we couldn't go farther and then paddled out, just as the wake of an ore boat a mile away came crashing into the cavern, waves that would have smashed us to a pulp and instead we sat in the canoe and watched the waves pounding into the cavern and said nothing, there being nothing to say. And eventually I turned 50, which is too old to die young. Whenever I relive those close-call moments, all regrets vanish, all complaints evaporate. I survived to do hundreds of shows and when the audience laughs it feels like a good reason to go on living.

And I've come to relish writing more and more especially after the Delete key was invented, which ranks with Gutenberg's movable type in the annals of human progress. Back in the typewriter age we had liquid white-out but Delete enables you to remove whole pages of your own gloomy nonsense. I gave up dark writing for the simple reason that it fails to hold the interest of the writer. It's boring.

Gloom is just like carbuncles:
Yours is the same as your uncle's
Whereas the hilarious
Is wildly various
Like the wildlife found in the jungles.

I left Minnesota and friends and family in 2018 after Minnesota Public Radio, fearful of a shakedown scheme by two former employees, threw me out in the street, a miserable mistake on their part, and at 76, I needed to put it behind me and so we took up residence in Manhattan where I enjoy anonymity and Jenny loves the city and our daughter is nearby, so it was a smart move all around.

And when I stood in that gym watching her and my fellow autists leaping and dancing to the hits of my youth played by a man with a rope coming out of his head, I was so happy it made me cry just as I do in church when we sing about the awesome wonder of the world and the stars and the thunder *O Lord, how great thou art* and we old angsty Anglicans stand and raise our hands in the air at this Baptist revival hymn, we the overachievers transformed into storefront charismatics. It's quite a sight. It happened one morning with the chorus, *And I will raise you up, and I will raise you up, and I will raise you up on the last day.*

It was Easter morning, brass players up in the choir loft, ladies with big hats, and when the clergy processed up the aisle, the woman swinging the censer looked like a drum major leading the team to victory over death. Resurrection is not something we Christians talk about in the same way we talk about our plans for retirement, but it's right there in the Nicene Creed and in Luke's Gospel the women come to the tomb and find the stone rolled away and the mysterious strangers say, "Why seek ye the living among the dead?" This all hit me when we sang, "And I will raise them up," I raised my right hand and imagined my long-gone parents and brother and grandson and aunts and uncles coming into radiant glory, and I was surprised by faith and I wept. My mouth went rubbery, I couldn't sing the consonants. I stayed for the benediction, slipped out a side door onto Amsterdam Avenue, and headed home. Without the Resurrection, St. Michael's'd be just an association of nice people with good taste in music but when it hits you what you've actually subscribed to, it can blow your head off, me the author standing and weeping among stockbrokers and journalists and lawyers for God's sake.

This never happens at meetings of the American Academy of Arts & Letters up on 155th Street, writers and composers and painters and architects do not stand, singing, moved to tears: it simply does not happen. It happens at St. Michael's on 100th Street. I don't know if they do this at All Souls Unitarian over on the East Side, I think maybe they think about doing it, but hymns about inclusivity and tolerance and justice that leave Divinity out of it except as a beam of light or a rainbow or a starry sky—I'm sorry but that doesn't make New York adults raise their arms and weep. The Lord is great indeed. He is here among us, from the public housing projects to the castles of Central Park West, amid the honking and double-parking of delivery trucks, God is here and we are His, we of the Academy and also kids on the spectrum, jumping and dancing. This cheerful thought can get you through some dark days. My mother knew deep grief when she was six years old, a little sister died of scarlet fever, and soon after, her mother died, and Grace lost the memory of her mother, couldn't recall her voice, her manner, stared at snapshots of Marian trying to bring her to life, and it makes me happy to think of them reunited in happiness. There endeth my sermon. Go in peace.

2

The Mitral Valve

A few years after my parents died, I learned that I was lucky to exist at all. Grace and John married in scandal in 1937 after a five-year engagement during the Depression when Grace was a nurse in Minneapolis and John was trapped on the family farm thirty miles north. His mother needed him, his father having died. And then one day the double team of horses he was driving, hauling a wagonload of cow manure to spread on a field a quarter mile away, bolted and galloped in a panic toward home and he hauled on the reins but couldn't control them. They raced into the farmyard and the turn was too sharp and the wagon overturned in the ditch, the hitch snapped, the horses stopped, exhausted, and John, though shaken and shat upon, was so elated by survival that he wrote Grace a long passionate letter describing what had happened—a fine passage of narrative prose—and then decided to deliver it in person and borrowed his brother Bob's Model A and drove to the city and the two sweethearts reconnoitered. Three months later she learned she was pregnant and she told John and they had to face her father who was a devout evangelical and therefore furious and denounced them for succumbing to temptations of the flesh against the teachings of their loving Savior who gave His life for them. Had he ordered her to a home for unwed mothers, my brother Philip might've been adopted by a wealthy family in Wayzata and gone to Yale and the two lovers driven apart by righteous condemnation but Grandpa was forced to forgive them, knowing full well that his own Marian McKay in Glasgow had been three months pregnant when he married her. This transgression was why they came to America, to escape the shame. To keep his secret safe, he had to forgive his fellow sinners. So Grace and John found a judge and married, and five years later, as she was sending John off to war, in the drama of saying farewell, perhaps forever, with their little boy and girl asleep in the next room of their rented house in Anoka, in her emotional turmoil she got careless and conceived me, an unnecessary child, and in August 1942, I emerged at Dr. Mork's Maternity Hospital on Ferry Street in Anoka. We won the war and Dad built us a house in the country and I went to school and became a writer and wrote a magazine article about a radio show and then started one of my own. I, who had no social skills at all, became a close personal friend of thousands of radio listeners, all of them invisible, a Brethren boy brought up to practice alienation as a spiritual duty who learned how to make listeners feel reassured. A marvelous fake. If you wrote this as a novel, nobody would believe a word of it. Not even "the" or "if." And then comes the kicker.

By the time I turned 59 and was due to die, the heart-lung machine had been invented and perfected, which made it possible for Dr. Tom Orszulak at Mayo Clinic to cut open my chest and sew up the mitral valve. A couple months later I went back for an echocardiogram and saw on the screen the gray silhouette of a fluttering flower, my repaired valve opening and closing, proof of how lucky I was, these little petals, once inaccessible, now operating on all pistils, thanks to skilled intervention by men and women who did not doze off in math and physics and biology, as I did, but paid close attention and felt a vocation. I am no spring chicken—chickens don't get echocardiograms—but I feel obligated in my remaining years to do sufficient good work to justify the men and women in white going to all that trouble and a couple decades later, by God, I'm still trying.

Longevity was a beautiful undeserved gift, I having smoked whole fields of tobacco and consumed barrels of alcohol while leading the sedentary life of a writer, a large ashtray full of butts by the typewriter. Later, I survived a stroke when a blood clot got blown into my brain a millimeter from the wiring that enables speech and mobility, a little clot that would've made me a mumbling stumbling dummy but it missed the bulls-eye. I put away alcohol when I was 60 because I often drank myself stupid and I dreaded the prospect of AA and sitting in a circle of folding chairs in a church basement on Tuesday nights with other men, talking about our emotionally distant fathers. So I gave up Glenlivet for ginger ale and my head cleared up and I could sit at a keyboard in the morning, not hungover, and produce interesting sentences. A sensible man chooses work over drink, though I'd taken to drink because it seemed, thanks to Fitzgerald, Hemingway, Faulkner, Cheever, et cetera, that inebriation was a badge of authenticity for a writer. You poured a tumbler full of bourbon to pacify the demons who animated your genius. But why seek more stupor when you've more than enough to begin with? And I discovered, as so many others have, that it's easy to stop drinking so long as you don't drink. Repeat that sentence, dear reader. Drinking is the problem. So don't. Enjoy Communion wine on Sunday and let that be the end of it.

And the reader pokes her head up from under the dining room table where I am writing this book and she says,

"Pardon me, but we're in the second chapter and I don't have any idea where you're going with this. Is this going to be a confessional or a book about cheerfulness? My parents were major fans of yours. Me, not as much, though I liked the detective in the Acme Building trying to find the answers to life's persistent questions. I did love the story about your grandma singing you to sleep with the song about little kids freezing to death in the woods. That was good. And the limerick about the old man of Bay Ridge who cried out 'Son of a bitch, I got up in the night and on came the light and I find I have pissed in the fridge.' But otherwise, there was an awful lot of meh, *if you know what I mean. But don't let me interrupt you. You're busy writing, which, at your age, is pretty amazing, so I'll let you get on with it, I just wanted you to realize that you're not alone, I'm here, and to be honest with you, and why not, the God stuff goes right by me and urging people to be cheerful flies in the face of reality, so if this is meant ironically, why not come out and say so?"*

"It's not," I said, but she was gone. I was so taken aback, I didn't get a good look at her. She had a pleasant voice and spoke very clearly like maybe she taught fourth grade.

L ife is good. I arise early and make coffee and sit
down to write for a few hours, as I am doing now,
and then Jenny walks in and sits on my lap and
I put my arms around her, and thanks to my evangelical upbringing that condemned carnal pleasure, I am
thrilled by this modest physical contact. I scratch her
upper back between the shoulder blades, and she sighs a
long legato sigh. She says, "Don't talk to me, I just woke
up" so I don't. But what is there to say? The polar ice cap
is melting, people are shooting each other for no good
reason, authoritarianism is raising its horny head, people
sit in Congress who thirty years ago couldn't have been
elected county weed inspectors, and yet the quotidian
pleasures are forever beautiful because, on my third try, I
married well. She is the sister of my younger sister's high
school classmate who gave me her phone number. One
lucky phone call changed my life.

I met her in New York City in the spring of 1992,
we had lunch at Docks on Broadway and 90th after she
returned from an orchestra tour of Southeast Asia and
Japan. She'd left Minnesota in her late teens to live the
life of a freelance violinist in New York, knowing that
in order to play Brahms and Tchaikovsky you may need
to live in a little walk-up apartment with roommates,
where drug addicts doze in the vestibule overnight and
the cockroaches are the size of hummingbirds. But she
loved classical music and took whatever gigs she could

get, the Three Tenors one week, then riding a bus around mid-America to play one-nighters of *La Bohème*, subbing in Broadway pits, enduring periods of near poverty but not giving up. She learned to live on ramen noodles when necessary and took long walks to ward off the blues, and she was very upbeat about it all. She was 35 now and didn't regret a bit of it. This was all quite new to me: I found poverty demeaning, she did not, to her it had a purpose. I found this fascinating.

She came to my 50th birthday party in August, we married three years later, our daughter was born in 1997, and now, thanks to God's mercy and modern medicine and despite my prodigious bad habits, here we sit on the front porch of a little house on a cove of the Connecticut River, drinking coffee, watching a family of foxes playing tag on the lawn, our daughter Maia asleep upstairs, a quiet Sunday, August 7, 2022, my 80th birthday. No fuss, no fluffery. No gifts. Life is the gift. No birthday cake: it might burn the house down. I feel like the luckiest man in my age bracket. Diligence is all well and good but thank God for wild good luck. The best and the brightest studied math and made careers in the fast-moving frontiers of science where obsolescence sets in around age 35, and I did a radio show that, because it was nostalgic, defied change, and thus did the turtle outrun a great many hares.

It's August, I now am fourscore
And before I go out the door
As a non sequitur,
One more dance with her
And I'll mix us a nice metaphor.

So much hangs on that first lunch at Docks. If she'd looked at me and said, "I'm sorry but I can't stay long, I have to meet a friend," it would've left a deep canyon in my life, but she was very cheerful and had a good appetite and talked about her recent orchestra tour of south Asia and the climb up a steep hill to a temple and the monkeys who were adept at picking the tourists' pockets and lunch lasted for three hours and here's the result. A loving partnership of two independents with a few crises resolved and steering a steady course. The love affair, the daughter, the thirty-year history, all hang on a two-minute phone call, she on 102nd, me on 90th. Mine was a landline, the phone with a curly cord on the pantry wall. I was ready to leave New York and go live in the woods of Wisconsin. I'm not a New Yorker, I don't have enough opinions, I'm not picky about food, and if someone mentions Taylor Swift, I wouldn't say, "Let me tell you about the time I met Taylor Swift," even if I had met her. But here I am, residing, paying taxes, a MetroCard in my billfold, a registered Episcopalian, thanks to her. You don't find a violinist in the Personals who's looking

38

for an older lover, preferably a grim-faced writer with nondescript hair. It's pure luck.

I walk to 83rd to mail some letters and pass couples dining under awnings on the sunny side of the street, greenmarkets with their goods out on wooden pallets. No alleys here so everything happens out on the street, goods are trucked in, garbage out, you're walking along a loading dock with flower boxes. Elders perch on the brownstone steps and gaze on me with a judicious eye but they see little kids come trotting along and their hearts melt. I pass a little Victorian firehouse, one truck wide, wedged in the row of brownstones holding off the invasion of high-rise condos. A papa stands on the corner, embracing one tall daughter, then the other, both carrying gifts, heading for a party. Skateboarders swoop along the bike lane, helmeted kids on scooters. Brisk walkers passing us amblers, people walking their dogs who watch for other dogs to talk to. The sun is out and there is good feeling everywhere I look. There are writers in this neighborhood busy writing accusatory memoirs or nonfiction about heinous acts by vicious men, so it's up to me, a tourist, to pay witness to public happiness, the old couple feasting on fettucine in the sunshine, the guardian elders, the proud papa, the gallant skateboarders. It's the human comedy where people are linked by friendship and family, the weak are protected, venality is resisted, and the ordinary is relished.

At 81ˢᵗ, I go down into the subway and the downtown train rolls in and I squeeze into the car without bumping anyone and we rumble south, six complete strangers within a few inches of me, everyone in his or her own space, avoiding eye contact, thinking their own thoughts. I once saw John Updike on a downtown C train, the good gray man of letters grinning at the life around him, and once on the same train I saw the master trumpeter Wynton Marsalis. Nobody bothered either one of them and they rode along with us commoners. Both times, I tried not to stare. "On any person who desires such queer prizes, New York will bestow the gift of loneliness and the gift of privacy," said E.B. White. "No one should come to New York to live unless he is willing to be lucky."

I'm old but I'm not done with being lucky yet. I'm done with radio. Done coveting prizes. The arts are all about prizes, the Pulitzer, Booker, Schnooker, Emmy, Tony, Sammy, Jimmy. It's your Get Out Of Anonymity Free card. You win one and it's stuck to your name for the rest of your life: *The Sammy-winning psalmist will hold a seminar on Saturday* and you're miserable that you won the Sammy for your 22ⁿᵈ psalm, which was a sham and a piece of schlock and you weren't even nominated for your 23rd, which was seminal and sensational. I'm done with all that but I'm not finished with work, not nearly. I am ambitious to realize my ideal monologue, which would be 90 minutes nonstop semi-improv and include bit of old songs and passages of poems and sound like a wise lunatic who is also piss-your-pants funny. I sit down to write every morning and that is the grand prize. Except that morning I turned 80, I sat on the porch in Connecticut with the woman I love and saw even more clearly how lucky I am. I'm a leaning tower of good fortune.

I heard the church bells that Sunday morning and might've put on my shoes and gone, but I felt blessed already. Dancers wear out their cartilage and have to open a studio over the dry cleaners and teach tango and foxtrot to lumbering flat-footed klutzes, guitarists get carpal tunnel syndrome and regress from progressive jazz to "Go Tell Aunt Rhody," decent singers have large aspirations and become crappy songwriters, painters inhale toxic fumes and must take jobs at Walmart, composers wheedle an NEA grant to compose an orchestral suite called "Passages" that is performed once at Yale and everyone is glad when it's over and the premiere is also the derriere, but we prose writers are unsinkable. I went for a walk in February around the Central Park Reservoir and I banged my head hard on a low-hanging tree limb and knocked myself down and I came home and started writing a novella about a cold day in Minnesota when my metabolism got so low they thought I was dead and I awoke lying in a coffin listening to myself being eulogized and rose up to correct the eulogist on a few facts, and it was a fine beginning of a book I plan to finish as soon as I'm done with this one.

3

Glossary

Climate is not a factor in cheerfulness. Yes, winter can be wearisome, shoveling wet snow and throwing it up over the ten-foot snowbank and taking little sliding steps to avoid falling, but spring can be too, cherry blossoms can trigger rare allergies that put you on powerful medications that suppress your sense of humor. Summer is assumed to be exhilarating, but it often falls short and you think, "It's a beautiful moonlit summer evening, I'm drinking a dry medium-bodied sauvignon blanc with subtle herb accents, a light palate, and a refreshing finish and I ought to be happier than I am." Autumn is a big letdown too. The crisp October evenings bring memories of Miasma College and Heather, the girl who sat in front of you in French and was in your conversation group and who corrected your pronunciation in a way that scarred you for life.

No, "bad" weather is what promotes cheerfulness, if you ask me. A tornado that rips your neighbor's roof off, high winds and 15 inches of rain that devastate a nearby town and you open your home to refugees, a raging blizzard accompanied by thunder and lightning—natural disaster gives focus to your life. Nature is trying to depopulate us. We don't need to think long-term, we just deal with how to get through today, what to wear, what to eat. Self-pity declines. No need to sit around and anguish over what to do with your life. Instinct tells you. You're a mammal. Stay warm. Stay close to the food supply. Make babies. Make extras in case the wolves get one. And lighten up. As Mark Twain said, "The best way to cheer yourself is to try to cheer someone else up," and he's been doing it now for a century and a half.

Cheerfulness is a choice. When you feel sour, take a shower, brush your teeth, fix a cup of ginger tea and while it steeps do some dance steps, and you'll feel a fraction better and from that fraction you can go on to become a featured attraction. I'm old and my legs are stiff and I am more out of touch with pop culture today than I am with Tanzanian politics but every morning I choose between Anxiety, Bitterness, Cheerfulness, Dread, Ennui, and Forgetfulness, and C is the correct answer. It's a new day, I have work to do, my beloved is here, the coffee is on, so I choose C. My knee hurts from when I tripped on Amsterdam Avenue and crashed to the pavement but a man ran up and helped me up and put an arm around me and asked three times if I was okay. I am okay. Why imagine otherwise?

Happiness is something else, it's more circumstantial: I write a long account of a trip to New York with my dad when I was 11 and suddenly the screen goes black. The battery ran out of power. I plug it in and a minute later, there's the story recovered from the darkness. Some genius designed a circuit that forgives dumb mistakes. I'm happy about that. In 1985, *Lake Wobegon Days* got a lovely front-page salute in the Sunday *Times Book Review* and the sales wiped out whole forests in Ontario. It made me wildly happy for days. A handsome version of my face was on the cover of *Time* the week I went to my 25th high school reunion and for the first time in my life I felt like a success story.

As a young writer, I looked down on bestselling books and celebrities but when it happened to me it made me happy. Other writers were welcome to resent my success and I did attempt to maintain a humble demeanor but now, years later, I can admit to being very very happy. Now my happiness comes in smaller doses. As the husband of a quasi-vegan, I cherish my rare opportunities to hunker down by a blazing fire and hack at a half-raw hunk of animal flesh and feel the bond of kinship with

Hrothgar and Ecgtheow, and look at each other and say, "Handlian sæliglic!" Happiness, in other words. And also at U of M hockey games, when our team scores and we stand and bellow "M-I-N-N-E-S-O-T-A!" I never get to do this in New York. I only bellow at Mariucci Arena. It makes me happy.

oy is for angelic beings; it's why they exist. Angels don't worry about aging or their complexions, don't suffer from irregularity, they just praise God with joyful anthems, period. Joy is also for children: my wife took a video in Central Park after an 18-inch snowfall, New York apartment kids on a snowy hill shrieking for joy as they slide down the slope on saucers and sleds and plastic sheets and scraps of cardboard. Christmas is joyful for us on Christmas Eve at St. Michael's and the sanctuary is packed, happy Manhattan children among us, fervently wishing for snow, and we sing *O come all ye faithful, joyful and triumphant* and the acolytes process up the aisle, tall and solemn teenage girls in white raiment bearing majestic candles with tremendous dignity that is astonishing, coming from 17-year-olds, and we all know the words of the anthem and there is triumph in our voices, which is rare for New Yorkers, we're accustomed to confusion and irony and fear of being struck down by a kid on an e-bike running a red light, but in this moment, sweetly singing o'er the pews, we actually sort of mostly believe in the impossibility that the Creator of the infinite, of galaxies a trillion light years away, came to this tiny planet in the form of a male child because He loved us so dearly He wished to take mortal form and suffer as we do.

By rights, it should be a midnight service. It used to be, but we're older now, so it's at nine. And toward the end, they turn out the lights and we stand, lighted candles in hand, and sing *Silent night, holy night, all is calm, all is bright,* and the thought of calmness on the Upper West Side is transformative, and the holy infant so tender and mild, and against our nature we weep, I weep, my mouth can hardly form the familiar words, I weep for joy, all of the trash of Christmas is wiped away, Frosty and Rudolph and the chestnuts and Tiny Tim, and we feel God's love for us, and we walk home down Amsterdam Avenue, transported by the faith, and the next day it's the usual, we open our stockings, peel our Christmas orange, look at the twinkly tree, eat Swedish meatballs with lingonberries and go for a walk. Our daughter FaceTimes her friends. Jenny works on a jigsaw puzzle. I work on my book about cheerfulness.

Blissfulness is brief; it comes along and you hope for more and then your cat Willow goes into hospice and a trombonist moves into the apartment below, which drives herds of cockroaches up the heating vents and your upstairs neighbor, in rushing off to JFK to fly to France, left his shower running and the super doesn't have a key and your kitchen ceiling crashes to the floor and the fire department cannot break the door down for water, only for fire. There is blissful ignorance, I suppose, but I know nothing about it, so far as I am aware. My father was a postal worker, a federal employee, not easily moved to bliss, but fresh sweet corn from the garden made him very happy. It was 30 seconds from stalk to boiling pot, husked en route, and he took three ears, buttered and salted them, and ate them laterally and because there were no words to describe hot fresh buttered corn, he was silent except for the crunching. He sometimes felt similarly about fresh-picked strawberries. He would've gladly planted corn instead of a lawn. Grass was about respectability. He preferred blissfulness.

I once spent a semi-blissful week in a pink stucco 1929 hotel in La Jolla, my wife reading on a chaise under a palm tree, our daughter swimming laps in the pool, me looking out on the Pacific where sea lions fraternize and waves crash on the rocks. A seagull perches on the balcony rail watching me eat my cereal and I toss him a raisin and he catches it. This almost never happens back on the frozen tundra where nature makes serious attempts to kill us. In paradise, it's Live and Let Live.

Some of our relatives moved to California when I was a kid and had an orange tree in their backyard. They visited us in June, wearing pastel outfits, driving cars with enormous tailfins, and their Christmas cards said "Happy Holidays" and didn't mention Jesus, which led us to believe they may have become Unitarians, meanwhile we endured brutal thirty-below nights and praised God for His goodness and mercy. Adversity draws you closer to the Lord, it's been shown time and again. Bliss leads you to believe He is unnecessary.

ubilation is rare but I remember it from the Cyclone roller coaster at the Minnesota State Fair when I was 16 and my girlfriend Corinne dared me and so we did. It was more than transformative, it was redemptive. I experienced a level of terror and out-of-body pleasure compared to which the drugs I tried in college turned out to be a letdown.

Corinne and I came back in a daze of pleasure and we lay in a pile of leaves by the river and we kissed and necked and ignored her mother calling her name, and we slipped our hands into each other's clothing and I knew it was wrong but I loved it with my whole heart. She was a wonderful kisser for a girl who got straight A's and was fluent in German and headed for Carleton College. She wanted me to kiss her everywhere and I tried to please her and then her dad came looking for her and I came home around 11 p.m. and my mother was at the door, wanting an explanation, so I made up a story in which I was hitchhiking home from Anoka and was picked up by an Army vet named Frank, who was drunk because his wife kicked him out of the house. He was a veteran of D-Day, landed at Omaha Beach, lay in a foxhole and two of his buddies fell on top of him, both dead. I told this story over my shoulder, avoiding eye contact, as I put my stuff away and made a sandwich and went to the toilet. Frank was a good man fallen on hard times, lost his job at General Mills, his wife said she was "sick of his mess," and now he was too drunk to drive so I drove him back to the Pierce Motel in Anoka and I hitchhiked back home. I had never lied in such extensive detail as this and it was all to defend a girl's reputation. She said, "What was his last name?" I didn't know; he hadn't told me. "What did he look like?" "He was short, unshaven, wore wire-rimmed glasses and a fedora." I told it so well that I got emotional about the fictional Frank and what might happen to him now. My mother accepted this fable though surely she had her doubts but I got home free and when you lie successfully to your mother, you cross a bridge to independence. I'd already crossed one with Corinne and now from the vantage point of 80, I see this day as transformational and redemptive both, a rare combination. Having escaped death on the Cyclone rocketing around on an elevated track on a flimsy wooden frame assembled by drunken carnies, many of them ex-felons, I had dived into the darkness of carnal delight with a friendly girl who said, "I don't want to get you in trouble," which I found exciting, the prospect of trouble, the fact that I had my hand up under her shirt and we were kissing and she was sighing in a melodious way.

Corinne was one of the smartest girls in Anoka High and went on to find a more sophisticated boyfriend, maybe a braver one, and we remained friends until she committed suicide in 1986 in Lake Cayuga. I grieve for her still. The evening in the leaves is as vivid in my mind as if it happened last Saturday. I still think I could have taken her into custody and saved her life. I now try to remember her playing the piano, me sitting by her, singing "On the Road to Mandalay" *where the flying fishes play and the dawn comes up like thunder over China 'cross the bay.* I was lucky to have known her as long as I did and I have to leave it at that. God, be merciful and grant her peace.

Elation, too, is momentary: with bases loaded, two outs in the top of the 8th, our center fielder makes an incredible racing outstretched catch at the fence, killing the rally, and trots in toward the dugout, as we whoop and cheer and see it twice on replay and once you know the outcome, the elation is gone. What's really remarkable is the fielder's tossing the ball to the kids in the bleachers, a casual underhand toss that clearly says, "No big deal. That's what they pay me to do." I feel elation at the Metropolitan Opera, watching *Aida*, with the ridiculous Act II procession of triumphant Egyptians hauling wagonloads of defeated Ethiopians through a set the size of the grain silos of Omaha, with trumpet fanfares, four horses, an elephant, camel, ballet dancers, spear-carriers, priests, the Met chorus in their robes and sandals singing the march, which sounds good in Italian but the English is dumb:

We won the war and so we wear
The lotus and the laurel:
They smell good and we don't care
If you think the war was immoral.
(My translation.)

It's a four-hour show, including two intermissions with long lines of women desperate to pee, and when it ends, with Aida and Radamès locked in the tomb, singing their beautiful farewell to this earth, I feel elated to be able to go home.

Contentment is so sweet: you sit with the family around the Sunday dinner table and everyone is more or less gainfully employed, nobody is under indictment for tax fraud or in chem-dep rehab, nobody believes immunization is the work of Satan, and your grandchildren eat with a knife and fork and don't use foul language in your presence—the needle on the normality index is right smack in the middle. It's lovely and it also makes you uneasy, anticipating the crisis that will break the spell, the softball that smashes through the window and knocks two bottles of pinot noir to the floor ruining your priceless 1876 Navajo carpet, the firetruck that pulls into your driveway—called to a fire on Elm Street and this is Helm Street but before they get the spelling right they've dragged an eight-inch hose up to the second floor and blasted water into Jimmy John's bedroom where he was looking at porn on TV and they hit him with a hundred gallons of cold water and sent him into treatment for shame for who knows how long, and Sundays will never be the same. Poor J.J. will develop an Excedrin dependency and drop out of school due to diarrhea and take up with a girl named Diane who demands you call her Douglas Fir. Why would a nice young woman identify as a tree? No, you know perfectly well that contentment is unnatural, it leads to trouble, like Hawaii; you spend a week on Maui and your life goes to pieces, you need to get back to Hoboken and your horrible neighbors and the smell of burning asphalt and the sound of sirens.

Gaiety is a lovely word that used to mean "inexplicable high spirits such as singing in the rain" and then it just meant Bob and George, but that's okay by me. "Gaiety," to my way of thinking, involved dressing up and a certain sort of frivolity, and cheerfulness can be easily accomplished by ordinary people in everyday outfits.

Glee tends to be cruel, the students' reaction when the college chaplain gives the invocation at Baccalaureate and passes gas so that his gown billows up behind him and his wife cries, "Oh, my God!" and the organist collapses on all four keyboards and it sounds like the torpedo hitting the *Lusitania* and all the sophomores snicker but for many of them, this will be the highlight of the year before they drop out and pursue a career in valet parking. Their glee will soon turn to gloom whereas His Flatulence will schmooze his way into the presidency of a small college where he'll sit in magisterial splendor and pen thank-you notes to generous donors.

I never saw a chaplain fart but whenever begowned

men take the stage, I hope for it, or that the great man's gown will be a size too large and he will walk up it and rip it in half and bend over to pick it up and we'll see his distinguished crack. Any time the noble and anointed take the stage, we hope for a mishap. That's one reason people sit in the front row. So they can see the dean whisper to the poet laureate who looks down and says, "Oh, God" and zips up his barn doors. I once gave a speech to Phi Beta Kappans at Harvard. As I was introduced, Helen Vendler leaned over and said, "Your shoelaces are untied." I said, "I know." I stood up and gave my remarks, walking to and fro, and the Kappans watched my every step, anticipating the crash as I recited Shakespeare, Cummings, Dickinson, Burns, Mary Oliver, and several sonnets of my own. I took long strides, laces trailing, and I had an attentive audience, though in the end glee was denied.

Triumph is surely related to glee but we don't use the word anymore. Once it was associated with Roman generals riding into captured provincial capitals and taking their pick of the local peasant women but it became hyperbolic when it was attached to a motor vehicle—it lost its *umph* and fell into disuse. Same with **exultation**—too fancy, too formal. A music critic might use it in a review of the Berlin Philharmonic playing

Beethoven but anyone who turns to you and says, "I feel so exultant," you'd immediately mark down as off-kilter.

Delight is of course delightful. I have great-nieces who are a delight, one is seven and dwells half the time in her imagination and with no effort turns a Minnesota living room into *Arabian Nights,* and it's wonderful and astonishing but also exhausting for the grown-ups. I felt delight once in church on a Sunday in January when a woman stood up to read a passage from the prophet Micah, including "O my people, remember what happened from Shittim to Gilgal that you may know the saving acts of the Lord." I'd noticed it in the bulletin, waiting for the service to start, and remembered how much I'd enjoyed that passage when I was 13, wishing one of the Brethren elders would read it aloud in Bible study, but it never happened, and now I was delighted, waiting for our reader to proclaim it. I could sense her trepidation. She approached "Shittim" very cautiously. This was not in a back alley somewhere, this was in St. Mark's Cathedral in Minneapolis, marble angels looking down, and she very carefully pronounced it "shi-team," as if it were French. I mean, "Shittim" is shittim, no shit. But she had been dreading this for an hour, wishing she were Unitarian, wishing it were Monday, afraid she'd accidentally pronounce it phonetically and an angel would come crashing to the floor narrowly missing a sexton who would lose his faith on the spot and turn to Scientology. It made me so happy. It was the highlight of the day. I have no recollection of the homily: some guy spoke English. Big deal. This was pure delight. I feel the exact same way about my sweetheart's bare shoulders. But if I had titled this book *Bare Shoulders*, it would've created expectations that couldn't be met. *Cheerfulness* is eminently attainable.

As for **euphoria**, it's best to leave it alone. Into each life some rain must fall and not only rain but also taxes, nausea, sadness, the taste of soap, mysterious incessant beeping, online fundraising appeals, hemorrhoids, allergic reactions to moisturizers, phone calls that put you on Hold to listen to repeated musical riffs that drive you mad and you decide not to bother with a cardiologist but to treat your heart arrhythmia with vitamin D3, and to achieve euphoria amid all of this may lead to you driving to a distant parking lot with $120 in an unmarked envelope and meeting a man named Rick in a Black Sabbath hoodie.

I once poured a line of white powder on a mirror and inhaled the stuff and nothing happened, no aura, no corona or vibe of vividity. The stuff I got for the extraction of wisdom teeth was the real deal but numbness is not a worthwhile goal. I prefer perceptivity. Cowboys in Wyoming used to sit in a saloon and compete to see who could pick up a silver dollar with your bare buttock cheeks off a hard wooden bench. A cowboy named Al Simpson was the champion and was said to have once picked up a dime. You couldn't do that if you were on euphoric drugs. Nor could you shoot straight. Nor, most likely, would you be able to tell a joke so it's funny, such as the one about the two penguins on the ice floe, one of whom says, "You look like you're wearing a tuxedo," and the other says, "What makes you think I'm not?" which, if told sloppily, people don't get. Lack of comic prowess reduces your worth in society to that of a hat rack or a floor lamp. You become furniture.

Cheerfulness is rare among writers, maybe because the failure rate is so high, or maybe because it's not taught in school. It went out of style in American Lit long ago. And the 75 percent of American writers who are down in the dumps give the rest of us a bad name. "Show me a hero and I'll write you a tragedy," said Scott Fitzgerald, who was disappointed that World War I ended before he could go to France and get shot. So instead he became the golden boy of 1920 with his first novel, *This Side of Paradise*, and he and Zelda ran around New York and the Riviera jumping in fountains and twenty years later he dropped dead, an expired celeb, at 44. And ever after him, American writers tried to be Euro and affected a heroic hopelessness, a traumatized turgidity tinged with suicidal sensibility, which was an act, like wearing a black beret and leading an ocelot on a leash. They ignored the millions of Europeans who made their way through Ellis Island to escape that very same hopelessness, hoping to find a sunny street of bungalows with well-kept yards and friendly neighbors.

Whenever I pull up to the drive-through window to pick up my Egg McMuffin, if I sense that the person who hands me the bag and growls, "Have a nice day" is an ambitious writer at work on an angry memoir about his suburban Siberia, I set it aside and go without. I don't want frustrated writers handling my food.

Something similar happened to pop music when the guitar took supremacy over the keyboard. Little Richard sat down at the piano in 1955 and tore the joint apart with "Tutti Frutti" *(A wop bop a loo bop, a lop bam boom!)* and even Lutheran teenagers jumped up and down but then Elvis (who could play piano) decided to be a cowboy and switched to guitar and that led to an endless stream of alienated loners and there went the ball game. The piano is a piece of furniture, it implies stability and home ownership, people gather around it and sing for pleasure, whereas the guitar is a weapon, an axe, and you sing bitter songs about wanting to leave town, which, with a guitar, you can do more easily than with a piano. You can't put a piano on the back of your motorcycle. Your mom wanted you to take piano from Mrs. Lindstrom but instead you bought a Mel Bay chord book and learned G, C, and D7 and wrote:

Sick of school, sick of family,
Breaking up with my girlfriend Emily,
Gonna hop on the bike with my Stratocaster,
Want to go fast, then go faster,
Life in Loserville is a mess,
Taking Highway 12 way out west,
Leaving no forwarding address.
Am I gonna miss you? Take a guess.

I've enjoyed my writing life though I have a large mausoleum of abandoned works and know what drought feels like, but I invented a town when I was 30 or so and have felt at home in it, hanging out with Bunsens and Krebsbachs, knowing them well enough to put words in their mouths. I've written for (as it turns out) enormous audiences and also for exclusive ones. My big success one week was a sonnet written at 5 a.m. on the day I suddenly realized was our wedding anniversary, an original sonnet written out in a clear cursive hand and set on the breakfast table for my wife to find. I heard her sigh with pleasure and she came into my workroom and threw her arms around me. One poem, one reader, one tight protracted embrace: an hour of work well spent. The rest of the day was all mishmash and goulash that wound up in the trash.

I think of cheerfulness as a Midwestern virtue. The food here is unremarkable, the cultural life is mostly imported, the scenery is nothing you'd drive long distances to see, and the people tend to be bland and seldom raise their voices in anger except to loved ones. But there is an everyday cheeriness that eases the strains and stringencies and the stone in your shoe. We may be intolerant but we're nice about it. As we say, "People—ya gotta love 'em," and we do our best to. And the secret of cheerfulness is, as Buddha and Jesus both said, to give up wanting material things. This fits the Midwest where there is less material to covet. This wisdom grows with age. Jesus said, "Think not what ye shall eat or what ye shall drink," and to make this clearer He married me to a strong woman and though this cucumber salad and glass of tap water are not what I was hoping for, not wanting is what makes me cheerful so I am. Some people have strong opinions about Kenyan vs. Guatemalan coffee. I'm okay with Maxwell House instant, black or with skim or half-and-half, Coffee Mate, or whatever. Coffee is not a transformative experience. I feel the same way about gender: it's your beeswax, not mine. Be binary, primary, grow an ovary, be Larry in January and Mary in February, be as contrary as you find necessary, become vegetary, it's no big deal to me, I meet you cheerfully and do not comment on the leafy stems growing out of your ears. You see yourself as a flowerpot and I trust that the roots don't go in too deep.

Every year, in late fall or early January, thousands of Minnesota snowbirds head for the airport and dump their parkas and mittens in the trash barrel and catch a flight south to a town with a Spanish name where they'll put on filmy garments and lie around a swimming pool under the palm trees where, having escaped the cold, the flatness, the oceanlessness, the scrutiny of neighbors, the inbred gloom of Northern people, the mockery of satirists like me, they feel at home at last, not admonished but cherished.

The sun is out, the sky unclouded.
Paradise, no doubt about it.
Lutherans, Catholics, Presbyterians
Sharing a paradise experience
For one month until we go ta
Resume suffering in Minnesota.

All is well for a couple weeks, maybe a month, and so, in search of permanent delight, perhaps euphoria, they up and leave Lake Wobegon for La Isla de las Delicias, abandoning their relatives and friends, Pastor Liz, the coffee club at the Chatterbox Café, their old classmates, the Christmas lutefisk lunch, the ancestors in the cemetery, the cousins who've studied family history going back to the 14th century, Ruth Harrison at the library—the entire moral foundation of their very being—and is it any surprise when these exiles fall into a leisurely dissolute lifestyle that leads inevitably to depression, drug dependency, devotion to demonic doctrines, dementia, and sudden demise in a sanitarium having signed over their entire estate to a satanist society? No. We tried to tell them but they wouldn't listen.

4

Three Cheers

It was their cheerfulness that propelled the Beatles to American stardom in 1964, a propulsive lightness after the bitterness of Dallas, the motorcade, the hero and his lady in the open car, the horror of the Zapruder pictures of her arm around him, then his brains blown out. Then Oswald seeing Jack Ruby approach in the city garage. The funeral cortege, the little girl and boy, the stricken widow. The sheer disbelief that led to years of aimless speculation about conspiracies when we had simply witnessed two murders. The old hack LBJ came to power, the grim tide of Vietnam deepened. And then this chipper Liverpool band flew into town, as much jug band and music hall as rock 'n' roll: they were white but could do black very nicely and with an irresistible backbeat, on *When I touch you I feel happy inside and it's a feeling that my love I can't hide, I can't hide—Ooooo.* My daughter and

I still sing this when we hold hands walking down the street. And *When I get home to you I find the things that you do can make me feel all right.* And *With you, whoa yeah, why do you make me blue?*

The three-part harmony was so impeccable and unaffected and even as the band turned a corner and was ambitious to be hip and got into psychedelia, even the dark stuff had a bounce to it ("I'm Looking Through You," "Nowhere Man").

Sixty years later, you stand around with elderly Boomers and they know all the words to a couple dozen songs. Sing *Well, she was just seventeen if you know what I mean* and all the 70-year-olds will join in and are delighted by the falsetto refrain. Sing *There are places I remember all my life though some have changed* and they'll sing through their tears. Who else wrote so many songs that stayed memorable so long? People adored them and they did concerts in stadiums where thousands of ecstatic girls drowned out the music and the band couldn't hear themselves and retired to the studio to escape the manic euphoria.

> *You know how long we've loved them.*
> *You know we love them still.*
> *We'll sing their songs a lifetime.*
> *We want to and we will.*

Bob Douglas was similarly cheerful, the mandolinist in the Powdermilk Biscuit Band in the early days of *A Prairie Home Companion,* who loved gospel songs, having grown up with them, even "It's G-L-O-R-Y to Know That I'm S-A-V-E-D," and he dove into bluegrass and swing tunes and played a driving backbeat on the fiddle standards, a dedicated devotee and serious folkie, but audiences get restless and earnestness only goes so far, and Bob's ace card was playing spoons. He kept them in his back pocket, ordinary kitchen spoons. No silver spoons, the tone was clanky. He held two spoons back to back an inch apart in his right hand, did elaborate rolls against the spread fingers of his left hand, and the rickety-tickety-bop glittery-flibbertigibbet shave-and-a-haircut drove the crowd wild. It never failed.

He worked hard to master a complicated instrument, the mandolin, but it was the parlor trick of spoonerism that blew them away—there's a lesson in humility here.

Bob wasn't eager to play the spoons, he was a mandolinist, not a clown, but he did it when it was needed and did it with a beautiful big smile, syncopating around, percussing hand-to-knee and off his forehead, bopping on the guitarist's shoulder, rapping on the knees of a kid in the front row, then the kid's father, he made solemn hippies whoop like third graders. Sometimes he'd switch to wooden spoons for the clackety tone. It was cheerfulness at work.

It was a lesson in show biz: do what you do but give the people what they want. Heather Masse, an educated jazz singer, could (and would, when needed) yodel for real, sing in a baritone blues growl. I myself, influenced by Bob Douglas, learned to recite the 87 counties of Minnesota in alphabetical order in one minute flat. It's impressive and the sound of it, *Aitkin Anoka Becker Beltrami Benton Big Stone Blue Earth and Brown* reminds me of Bob Douglas playing wooden spoons. When I hear myself slipping into the heartfelt and homiletic, I can always find my way to the 87, a minute well spent, and at the end, people yell, "Yes!" even if they've never been to Minnesota. As Judy Garland said, "Give the people what they want and then go have a cheeseburger."

Cheerfulness was what drove a junior senator from Illinois into the White House in 2008 against a much more experienced Republican opponent whom he easily beat and the Blackness of his daddy didn't matter much because the Democrat's smarts and wit and conversational style and cheerful cadences carried the day, the long pauses, the punchy lines that trailed off hilariously, and on Election Night, my mother, no Democrat, wept for happiness to see Barack and Michelle and the two little girls walk out on the stage in Grant Park in Chicago. Mother, married to a conservative whom she loved, didn't talk politics but she felt the righteousness of the moment. McCain was a hero; Obama was a newfound friend. His place in history will be argued long into the next century, but there was a spirit to the man that never got weary. He was, hands down, the funniest man ever to occupy the White House. (Maybe a First Lady or two was funnier but she kept it to herself.) He just got funnier as he went on. He enjoyed being our president and when he spoke to you, it landed and you felt his hand on your shoulder. His speech to the White House Correspondents dinner in 2016 was a string of big laughs. He said, "It's late. I'm running on CPT, which stands for Jokes White People Shouldn't Make. My brilliant and beautiful wife, Michelle, looks so happy to be here. That's called 'practice.'" Referring to the gentleman who would succeed him, he said, "Eight years ago I said it was time to change the tone of our politics. In hindsight, I clearly should have been more specific." (LAUGHTER.)

The president is the nation's Chief Mourner, it comes with the job: when terrible tragedy occurs, it's his duty to express grief and strike a hopeful tone, but here was something unique, a president enjoying being funny. "In my final year my approval ratings keep going up. The last time I was this high I was trying to decide on my major." Every word is in place, the timing is professional. He was soon succeeded by a man who couldn't tell a joke and never did, who'd gained attention by claiming Obama was born in Kenya. *How do you answer that? It's like someone calling him Rocky. That's not his name.*

That night Obama was beautifully funny for the maximum time permissible and then he did the obligatory salute to the role of the press, but when he was sailing through his best material he was the most American American in the room. Imagine, if you can, Nixon or George W. or McGovern or Hubert or Hillary at the podium, complimenting their brilliant and beautiful spouse who looks so happy to be here—it's called practice. But you can't. If you could, we'd be in a better place today. Let's give it up for Barack, the first prez to be able to say "let's give it up" and sound genuine. "Eight years ago, I was a young man full of idealism and vigor. And look at me now," he said. (LAUGHTER.) "Hillary once questioned whether I would be up ready for a 3 a.m. phone call. Now, I'm awake anyway because I have to go to the bathroom. I'm up." Six years later, Democrats brought back Barack and staved off disaster in the midterms. He was busy writing another memoir but the nation missed that voice. Republicans passed the two-term limit for the presidency because they didn't want another FDR, okay, understood, but when it stops a Barack and you get a Donald instead, a person has to wonder.

5

Old Age Is Worth the Long Wait. Definitely.

It's an excellent time: it's why your mother told you to look both ways before crossing the street and to chew your food thirty times before swallowing. It's why, when you drove drunk, you did so very very cautiously. The beauty of getting old is that I am no longer trying to find myself; I am here, this is me, forlorn mug and all. There is history written all over me and yet there is a secret child within. I don't dye my hair, don't use bronzer. I apologize for farting, I don't pretend it was someone else. I don't read inspirational books, thank you. My life is good enough. I no longer feel bad about being one of the few English majors who never finished reading *Moby-Dick* about old Cranky Pants with the wooden leg obsessed by the albino fish. I can forget about becoming multilingual and just stick with this one, a darned good language that has served me well. "C'est la vie," as we c'est. The burden of my pretensions lightens. Once I wanted to be a playwright and wrote a play and it was performed and it was dreadful and people were polite about it but the ambition passed like any other headache. I put politics behind me because I realize I have nothing to say that others haven't said better.

I used to spend an hour over the morning paper; I don't anymore. Newspapers are dismal places, full of government stuff and political opinion and lifestyle nonsense and of course crime but they never get to the heart of the story—what made that nice young man conspire with friends to kill his parents—and you read the paper and, aside from the weather, you get no sense whatsoever of what it was like to be alive in New York or Minneapolis yesterday—reporters are out to impress you with their hard-earned savvy, but nowhere is there a hint that people were happy, were amused by the life around them. You read the paper and you feel like leaving town. H.L. Mencken said, "A newspaper is a device for making the ignorant more ignorant and the crazy crazier." I glance at it so I can see what I don't need to know more about.

There are young people among us who argue that the country is systemically oppressive and corrupt, and there is no such thing as commonality, and comedy is a tool of oppression, but by the time they take over the country and institute righteousness, I'll be long gone, LaVonne, so there's no point in arguing with them, and meanwhile I can sit out on the terrace and look at the trees and tall grass in planters and listen to the mockingbird parents screech at me, warning me not to grab their fledglings who sit in the nest, beaks wide open, squeaking for food, just like our own daughter years ago, and I feel for them and stay at my end of the terrace and don't look their way. I want them to know that I eat no birds smaller than full-grown chickens, but they're right not to trust me. They know a carnivore when they see one.

I once gave my love an Italian cookbook for her birthday and she opened it and found recipes for leg of kid, eel, pork liver, braised snout, sweet-and-sour snout, and was so disgusted we entered into a vegan stretch for a month and a half. My fault. And then she saw how I was admiring her shoulder and upper arm and it made her uneasy and she bought a half pound of ground beef.

I'm not a hunter, I'm a writer, more interested in tillage than pillage. I'm a pacifist and observer in a greedy and violent world.

Classic, romantic, baroque,
Whether you sleep or are woke,
Remember this, Jack,
There's no turning back
From the fact that we live in a joke.

Eighty is not the end of the world but I can see it from here so I don't have long-range goals—there's just she and I, management and assistant, and the goals are survival and some degree of happiness, all the rest—synergy, networking, branding, having an impact, we're over that, now it's all about health and marble retention. Self-improvement is a lost cause. I once considered cosmetic surgery, a muscle implant around my mouth to enable me to grin, but once you start corrective surgery, you likely notice other flaws that require correction and a year later your belly button is in your armpit and your butt comes out lopsided so you have to wear orthopedic pants. Better to accept myself as is. So I do.

Back in my teens, my friends and I liked doing unkind impressions of geezerishness, the trembling hand, the shaky treble stammering voice, the long pause for the missing word, the loss of balance and the sideways lurch, and now I'm at the age I used to satirize and now maybe I am comical too but that's been my line of work for years and why change now?

I've gone out shopping for pants and come home with a dozen pens and a pad of paper. I have now and then roamed around the apartment searching for my glasses while my glasses were parked on top of my head.

"Why not hang your glasses on a chain around your neck?" she says.

Because I am not a reference librarian named Evelyn, that's why not.

Once we got up in the night to see a lunar eclipse and I put on a pair of sunglasses and she laughed like crazy. I once arose at 2 a.m. to use the bathroom and I urinated on my left foot, which did not escape her notice. Sometimes I walk into a room feeling gassy and tighten my anal embouchure to hold it in, which only produces more articulated farts, a whole string of them that sounds like "If wishes were horses then beggars would ride and the world be drowned in a sea of pride" and she smells natural gas, very natural, which makes her collapse in hysteria. I sit down and emit a sound like a walrus clearing its throat and she shrieks with laughter. It's a privilege to amuse her.

NOTE: Never marry someone who lacks a good sense of humor. She will need it especially if the marriage lasts and she winds up being married to an old man. And if it won't last, why go to all the trouble?

Just marry a desperately lonely man of 85 who has a pile of money and a bum ticker. As for men, don't marry a woman unless she is crazy about you. She'll likely have other eccentricities as well but you can put up with those if she truly adores you. So be adorable. In other words, look before you leap. This comes from a man who jumped in the dark and landed on rocks. Sharp rocks. Twice.

Nobody ever said to me, "Eighty is the new seventy." Because it's not, it's the home stretch. Most of the people living on earth when you were a child are now dead: that world is gone. You're walking into the dim vine-covered arcade with soupy organ music playing that maybe leads to eternal bliss or maybe a vast cloud of happy gas molecules. There are no U-turns allowed, a voice says, *Please keep moving*, middle-aged Boomers are pushing us and Gen X is pressing them. The poets told us to gather rosebuds while we may, that the flower that smiles today tomorrow will be dying, and it's all true, but *why in heaven's name is this happening to ME?* And then we discover that the uncertainty of tomorrow makes today rather beautiful. Stunning, in fact. Your feet touch the floor, a faint light shines through the blinds, the one you love sleeps next to you, you make coffee, the exotic smell of distant equatorial regions awakens thoughts of newspaper days, cafés in Copenhagen and hearing those sweet vowels, ø and ae and å, Al's Breakfast Nook in Dinkytown hearing the names Sartre and Camus and Kierkegaard, Mickey's Diner among the hungover drunks, early morning on the porch of the cabin at Cross Lake with Corinne, wondering if she wanted to be my girlfriend.

I have no sense of morbidity anymore. I thought about death enough when I was young. I had friends, Leeds and Roger and Barry, who died before they turned 21, a drowning and two car crashes. I got a whole life and they got only a slice, and not the best one. Back then, death was a terrible tragedy and at the age of 80 it feels like a definite trend among people I know. Mary, Margaret, Peter, Butch, Howard, Bob, Franz, Charlie. But I am alive today and that is an outstanding fact so make the most of it. When cousin Roger drowned at 17, trying to impress his girlfriend Susan, Mother sent me to swimming lessons at the Y, but the instructor was a terrible bully, so I went to the library instead, a wise choice, and I grew up to earn my way as a writer rather than as a professional swimmer.

Imagination! I read books and imagined writing one. I saw the soprano Ellie Dehn in a lead role in *Don Giovanni* at the Met, so commanding and fabulous onstage, and then was stunned to realize she's from my hometown, Anoka, an old railroad town on the Mississippi—I walked across the plaza and past the fountain in a state of wonderment (*How do you learn to be Donna Elvira in Anoka, Minnesota?*). She imagined her way there and got a couple breaks and there she was.

I wake up early and think, *Stand up, stand up for Jesus, ye soldiers of the cross. Help me put my feet back on the ground and I do appreciate your being round* and I tiptoe out to the kitchen. Maybe I do some stretches while I'm waiting for coffee but I avoid exercise. I have an aversion dating back to gym class in high school, having to do chin-ups and the running dive over the horse and forward roll, a ritual humiliation for a tall awkward person. So no gym for me. I take my meds, open the window, inhale the day, pour myself a cup. If I have a thought in my head, I scratch it on a pad of paper or tap it out on the screen and if it wants to be a paragraph or a page, I let it go free. *Some work in the morning may neatly be done that all the day after is never begun.* Work is crucial. The work comes first. When the Romans gave up farming for gluttony, they got so rotund their armor was too small and the Vikings poked a spear in them and let the gas out, *pffffffffffffft,* and it was Goodbye, Ovid, and Hello, Ole. I don't wish to go up in a cloud of gas so I sit and work. I'm well aware that an AI bot is available, which, if I gave it a prompt, could manufacture a passable passage about being 80 and feeling lucky and being in love and someday my vocation may go the way of clog dancing, canning, quilting, and cabinetry, but I go on writing, not knowing what else to do. An hour passes, two, three, I hardly notice, and then Jenny walks in and becomes my laptop.

The pandemic gave us a cloistered life, which is a good test of marriage, and the years of isolation made me appreciate her even more, her knack for finding things, her comic instinct, the raised eyebrow, the double take ("What did you say?"), her exquisite timing. Thirty years this funny woman has stuck by me—she whose eccentricities I am fond of, the bedtime routine of opening a window, running an electric fan, working a crossword puzzle, tuning in the BBC on headphones, all of which is necessary to induce sleep. She dozes off to news of fishing fleets on the North Sea and a campaign to preserve Shetland dialect. She is the designated worrier with dozens of us on her worry list and why not include fishermen and Shetlanders.

She is an inveterate hugger, whereas I am a shoulder patter. I haven't mastered the choreography of hugging, it feels grabby to me, possessive, like tackling. My father approached her on first meeting, his hand reached for hers, and she rose up and to his wonderment and alarm embraced him. My mother was delighted, after years of solemn Brethrenliness, to be squeezed. In the years since, at family funerals, the weddings of nieces, some evangelicals approach cautiously, wondering *Will it happen again?* And it does. She doesn't hug the plumber or the electrician, ditto the doormen and delivery boys. There is a protocol.

She is a straightener and neatener of things. I spill, she sponges. She walks into a room and if there is a little scrap of paper somewhere on the floor, a fragment the size of a postage stamp, she zooms toward it. Barefoot, she feels grit on a wood floor and goes for the vacuum. Once she looked at me and said, "Your hair is trying to do something it really shouldn't try to do" and that's about as harsh as she gets.

I am an apologizer and she's a forgiver: "Oh, that is so old," she says when I launch into remorse. She walks off her troubles in Central Park, six or seven miles' worth, part of which she runs, and she comes back exuberant with an account of people blowing big soap bubbles that landed gently on the reservoir and floated away, the Korean wedding by the lake and the man with Art Deco hair talking to his dog ("Girl! Fix your attitude!") and the excitement of the sea lions just before feeding time, and the conversation she overheard of a couple discussing whether to break up or get back together, it was hard to tell which, a crowd of people standing in a grove of elms, many with cameras with long lenses, looking up at Flaco the owl who escaped from the zoo, perched in a high crotch, a man in the meadow playing the Bach G minor unaccompanied sonata.

She is an uneasy flier and not fond of trains, but she loves to drive and shout directions at other drivers ("Get your fat ass over in your own lane, mister."). She beats me at Scrabble but is gracious about it. She creates salads that make me salacious. She rations my bacon cheeseburgers. She tells me if I look bedraggled. She is strict about squalor. She holds up a pair of black underwear she found in the couch cushions. It is a large pair with a slit in front. I weigh 220 pounds, she weighs half of that. "Whose is this?" she asks, rhetorically. She believes that disorder, if tolerated, leads quickly to chaos: allow a magazine to sit on the floor by the toilet and soon you've got dirty clothes on the dining room table, old bedsprings in tall weeds in the front yard and an old rusted-out Chevy up on blocks in the driveway, and the nice neighbors are leaving, replaced by ruffians. She is on guard for slippage, meanwhile she recycles paper, plastic, tin cans, everything except me. She needs me. She asks me to embrace her and also to scratch her upper back. She misses my presence in bed. She comes from a family of talkers and my people were not and sometimes we're like the Bob & Ray "Slow Talkers of America" sketch, in which Bob. Spoke. Very. Deliberately. So. As. To. Make. Each. Word. Perfectly. Clear. And Ray kept trying to finish Bob's sentences and finally blew up and wanted to strangle him. But she has come to appreciate quiet evenings, lying on a daybed, reading, me ten feet away writing at a table. A symbiotic marriage.

Her battle against clutter and chaos is a noble one. I once knew a couple men, both writers, whose lives jumped the tracks and fell into chaos and who became a shadow of themselves despite efforts to rescue them, spiraling down to the despair of their few remaining friends. Drug addiction was involved, depression perhaps, various bad choices of companions, and one drank himself to death in a faraway city, and the other recovered somewhat but permanently saddened and not the bright talent he once was. I also knew two men who lived lives of strict simplicity, austere, abstentious, militant in their focus on vocation, and faced with a choice between chaos and austerity, austerity looks awfully good. It does, however, require a vocation.

Chaos—a life driven by impulse, floating on the waves of the moment—is ever threatening to take us over the edge and it must be resisted, beginning with daily clutter and unrequited friendships and unrewarding habits such as TV. Entertainment that doesn't entertain but only distracts. I felt a great freedom when I banished it from my life. And then alcohol. The test of abstinence is: if you lose something and never miss it, you've gained. Abstention is worth experimenting with. Close this book and put it on a high shelf and if you aren't curious about what follows, probably you're as cheerful as you can be.

6

Old Man Thoughts

I'm an old writer, got the sedentary blues.
I need to take a walk soon as I find my shoes.
I got a good woman and she gave me a talk.
She said, "You're going to need a walker if you don't
get out and walk."
I know she's right, but what if I fall?
You go down hard when you're six feet tall.
I'll be lying there, dazed, my brain a mess,
And I'll never finish writing about cheerfulness.

My grandpa William Denham was a cranky old Scotsman but in a shoebox of old pictures, I came upon one of William weeding a strawberry bed and looking up at the camera and grinning. I don't recall him grinning ever. But here he was in Annabel Wright's garden, his wife, Marian, having died a few years before, and now William is courting the woman who is taking his picture, the lady he aims to marry. That is romance on Grandpa's face, carnal curiosity, call it what you will. He is looking for permission to approach the photographer and take her in his arms. The man fathered thirteen children; he can't be accused of lack of enthusiasm. There is brightness in his eyes and I see him more clearly now, kneeling by the strawberries, the man who did not stop at nine but fathered Grace, No. 10, and opened the door to my existence.

He died at 73. I am now seven years older than my own grandpa. I hold on to the railing while descending the stairs lest I descend ten of them suddenly all at once. I have age wrinkles on my inner upper arms. I don't read scary news stories such as "Interrupted Sleep May Lead to Dementia." I am astonished, having used outhouses as a boy, to walk into a men's lavatory and pee in a urinal and step back and it automatically flushes. The outhouse was premodern and having used one, postmodernism is startling to me. I remember the six-digit phone number, the party line, the wooden box on the wall with the little crank and speaking tube and earpiece hanging on a cord, and so the cellphone is amazing, the *Times* app, the map you can search for directions to the nearest stationery store, meanwhile I watch for curbs as one would watch for rattlesnakes. I have vision problems, poor hearing. I go to dinner at our friends' house and realize I've forgotten my hearing aids and so the conversation may as well be in Urdu and I try to produce appropriate facial expressions (keen interest, mild amusement, righteous disapproval) for the next three hours. And now I've read an article about hearing loss being connected somehow to Alzheimer's so there's that to think about.

Yes, there is a dark side to 80. I hang out with people my age and the conversation often turns toward hip replacements and unless you drop a china platter on the floor or the dog vomits up a meatball, you will hear about the relative virginity of French vs. Italian olive oils. And of course there's loneliness and guilt, a sense of meaninglessness—you wonder: why am I here? What did I come in the kitchen looking for? Why am I holding a spatula? But the moment passes, thanks to memory loss.

I felt my age last fall when I forgot my billfold in the back seat of a taxi and chased it for four blocks a month after my open-heart surgery. I knew I'd forgotten it the moment the cab pulled away, a red billfold chosen for its unforgettableness, and I ran out of horror at the thought of having to tell my wife and thereby raise the ominous thought of dementia, also the thought of having to replace the credit cards and call up Medicare and so I galloped after him, though it was not a gallop so much as an accelerated stagger, but thanks to a traffic jam I caught him and retrieved the billfold. I felt stiff the next day but it was worth it. Forgetting my billfold is on my

Prohibited list, along with falling, feeling dizzy, following a woman I've mistaken for my wife, and failing the doctor's memory test. So far, so good. The moral of the story: aging, though likely to be fatal, need not be dull.

Meanwhile, I am okay with being ignorant of celebrities whom everyone else knows, like Victor Wembanyama or Giannis Antetokounmpo. I don't know what crop tops are and don't care. A young relative holds up his phone and plays me his favorite song and I hear incoherent noise as he stands, stunned by genius. One less thing to occupy my time, now that I have so much less of it. I used to be a Vikings fan but then I read that fans of losing football teams experience a 20 percent drop in testosterone, which is cruel to contemplate, a game ends in defeat and your wife hugs you to comfort you and you think, "Oh no, let's not go down this road again." So I gave up football. My wife is grateful.

But these are trifles; I have a good life. Reaching 80 is worth the trouble.

I now accept that colorless hetero males have become fringe figures in American life and will likely be phased out in a few years, replaced by manufactured semen and better babies will come down the chute, no allergies, syndromes, or complexes, as the gender balance is adjusted to 90-10, women to men, making for a peaceful and rational world, with a few million CHMs kept around for heavy lifting, honor guards, garbage collection, and the disposal of dead rodents. Personally, I feel it is liberating to become peripheral and irrelevant: you are freed from the expectations of others, free to simplify your life, delete the stuff that makes no sense. I scratched college basketball, Florida vacations, expensive loud restaurants, science fiction, pocket billiards, the Book of Revelation, and broadcast journalism, and thus life is tidied up. As a young man, I practiced irony and saw pretense and arrogance wherever I looked, and now I see splendor and bravery and genius and kindness as the real story and have faith that the story will keep going. I am kind to strangers; I hold the door open for people except young women who might be offended and tell me to go to hell.

My friend Harry Reid, who grew up dirt-poor and fought his father to protect his mother and hitchhiked forty miles to go to high school, and wound up marshaling the Affordable Care Act through the U.S. Senate—I talked to him a couple months before he died and he was full of life and quoting Mark Twain: "I've lived through some terrible things in my life, some of which actually happened." Harry called me a modern-day Mark Twain and I said, "I'm twine, not Twain. You on the other hand could be his twin." Harry was lively right up to the end, a decent stand-up guy. May he rest in peace and rise in glory.

As for me, I'm on the verge of decline and surely decline can be hard. Old pitchers get shellacked one day because the slider won't slide and the next spring they're selling used Toyotas and dealing with being former. Old writers slip into self-parody and that's when people give them lifetime achievement awards. Old politicians get a book contract and realize it's hard to make a coherent memoir out of forty years of attending meetings. Movie stars take bit parts as befuddled neighbors or psycho-pathic retirees. Old pop stars play small casinos, the kind with the slot machines alongside the stage and there's no dressing room, just a hallway where they hang out with fans they don't want to know. Old humorists write a book about aging, the very thing nobody wants to know more about. That's how it goes.

But decline needn't be precipitous. And gradual decline can be disguised as a stylistic choice. You're not slowing down, you're allowing your chi to find its Tao. My wife's mother was a feminist so my wife is confident in hardware stores and issues instructions to painters and plumbers who glance over at me and ask, "Do you need to run this by him?" and she says, "No, he's a writer." Authorship is a perfect disguise, incompetence posing as otherworldliness.

My mother, Grace, was lucid to the end though sometimes she conversed with her sisters Elsie and Jean who were gone from the world but still clear in her mind, and she died at 97, recognizing us children, comprehending what we said, looking exhausted, and when I said, "Would you like to lie down?" she said yes. We sat around her bed for two days, singing hymns to her, the more joyful ones, holding her hand. Ten feet away was the kitchen where the carnivals of canning took place, the kitchen like a boiler room, billows of steam from the cooker, teakettles boiling— hot water to skin the tomatoes and sterilize the glass jars, slaving away to maintain our lives. As a child, I worried that maybe canning was a sign that we were poor. Our neighbors were not canners. The dread of the stigma of poverty stuck with me until I went to college and actually was poor and took it as a point of pride. My mother believed in Christmas, the festival of generosity, of good cheer and a light heart in the face of darkness and adversity, and now she lay small and frail, drifting away in the downstairs bedroom of the house Dad had built seventy years before. It was more or less as she wished to go, gently, at home, among loved ones. I sang to her. *When peace, like a river, attendeth my way and sorrows like sea billows roll, whatever my lot Thou hast taught me to say, It is well, it is well with my soul.*

She was enclosed in a fine bronze casket and buried

next to Dad in the Trott Brook cemetery just north of the Keillor farm where she fell in love with him, though I sort of wish she would've landed in the Pioneers Cemetery at Cedar Avenue and Lake Street in Minneapolis, not far from her childhood on Longfellow Avenue. Mother wasn't a country girl and at Trott Brook she is surrounded by farm wives, many of whom she was not comfortable around, women who could drive truck and use firearms and handle a chainsaw. Pioneer is the cemetery where I believe she went one night in the fall of 1936 with John and lay on a blanket in the grass and got pregnant. Anyway I've bought two plots at Trott Brook near my parents, one is for my ashes to be deposited in a cardboard box and the other is to be left vacant for lovers to sit down on. My tombstone will say, "And He will raise them up at the last day," but if anyone wants to lie down, that is fine by me.

7

Guilty of Good Fortune

The goddess Themis, holding her scale and weighing compassion against justice, is likely to be tough on me since I've avoided suffering so assiduously. I neglected my teeth, which should've rotted to black stumps long ago but still chew pretty good. I never went to war, never got into an actual fight in which someone slugs you, didn't serve in the Peace Corps, wasn't a Freedom Rider, never taught third grade. I didn't do stand-up comedy until I was in my sixties and the audience was too and nobody heckled, and when romances went south, I went north, slipped quietly away, unable to face a woman's fury. I accepted women's authority in behavioral matters, since I had learned good behavior from my mother and my aunts. I assumed I was wrong and it was too painful to discuss so I didn't. Four breakups with less discussion than if deciding where to dispose of a sofa.

Writers should be intimately familiar with despair and have visited its depths and I'm not because I didn't so I don't pretend to. So justice dictates that I go down hard, perhaps trip on a log in the woods and break my back and be chewed to death by beavers. Or at least be zapped by a brain seizure that wipes out my predicates and prepositions and I talk garbled talk and am shoveled into a Home for the Inarticulate. Fair is fair.

But I had no intimations of conclusivity that August 7th morning on the Connecticut River, turning 80, rather a sense of perpetuity. I had a date with a cardiac surgeon, Dr. Dearani at Mayo, on August 25th when he'd open up my chest and repair the tricuspid valve and replace the mitral valve. The 2001 repair was leaking badly, so I was getting only half the blood as normal. Time to recover the bloom of youth.

Facing surgery did not lead to thoughts of death whatsoever. I can't imagine dying at the Mayo Clinic because everyone there is so mannerly. A Russian gulag, yes; Miami, maybe; Mayo, no. Dr. Dearani was an ace surgeon and also a serious jazz saxophonist—a surgeon with soul. He explained my chronic left-sided diastolic failure and the ablation of the papillary muscles and posterolateral left ventricular annulus and how they'd repair the tricuspid valve while closing off the atrial appendage and replace the mitral valve with a 31mm porcine bioprosthesis. I took notes; I like when a doctor explains things fully, it shows respect for the patient. "Porcine," he explained, does not refer to porcelain, but to a valve belonging to a pig. I was all right with that. I do hope that donor pigs are well-treated, not fed slop from a trough but served generous portions on plates and transported aboard buses, not in livestock trucks. A pig whose heart valve saves your life should be shown due deference. But I am not likely to organize a campaign in their behalf.

My generation, the pre-Boomers, came of age in the afterglow of World War II, believing in victory and prosperity even as rock 'n' roll provided the pleasure of rebellion without consequence. We rode around the countryside freely, no worry, observing grown-up life, inventing games—one boy throws a tennis ball at a flight of stairs, the fielders must field it, imaginary runners run the bases, scores are kept—we put on coronations and conducted criminal investigations and carried out executions, fought the Indian wars, all of us wanting to be Indians, and made ice forts and lobbed grenades at each other, dammed up the spring melt in the gutters, swam in the river, raced bikes down a hill. And we picked up odd jobs for farmers and spent our earnings on Baby Ruths and Butterfingers at Yaklich's grocery. "See a penny, pick it up, and the rest of the day you'll have good luck," we said, and so we did. And we were lucky.

Benson School was not a locked fortress; back then strange men didn't go into schools and shoot little kids, we never imagined such a thing. Our bikes were parked, unlocked, by the front door. In Minneapolis, when I was 15, the three O'Kasick brothers set out to rob a Red Owl grocery store, and they killed a cop, fled to a game preserve north of Anoka where a posse tracked them down and killed two of them. This was an enormous event and my friends and I discussed it for months and still remember it. Now, multiple shootings are a daily occurrence in Minneapolis and hardly noticed and schoolchildren are trained in how to take cover.

Medical advances came along just as we needed them, and Medicare to pay for them. Post-1980, popular music went into decline so we were free to devote ourselves to the arts and write our memoirs. We are lucky to have been born in such a favored spot in history, any later and we wouldn't know how lucky we are, any earlier and we'd be deceased.

I appreciate my good fortune now. My elder friend the poet Robert Bly had a bestseller *Iron John* back when there was a men's movement but it disappeared due to gender fluidity when masculinity liquified and pissed itself away and men were no longer required to be iron unless ironically but men's militias formed waving shooting irons and needed to be put behind steel bars, none of which profited the prophet. Robert had a great book of poems, *Silence in the Snowy Fields,* but nobody south of Iowa reads books that speak admiringly of snow and silence so it sat between Berryman and Bukowski on the top shelf of the Poetry section, too high for normal readers to reach.

My life has been a Sunday picnic by comparison. I read poetry on the radio and once a woman heard my voice in the grocery store inquiring about the prune juice and she whispered, "I loved the Cummings poem. *Since feeling is first, who pays any attention to the syntax of things will never wholly kiss you.*" This sort of thing doesn't happen to most men, not in grocery stores. I believe I am the only person ever to sing a sonnet about cunnilingus with the New York Philharmonic at Lincoln Center. Some people may have done it at a Philharmonic party at a horn player's home but I did it in front of a paying crowd. I once gave a reading of original limericks to the American Academy of Arts & Letters, with some of the limericized in the crowd:

For the sage humorist Calvin Trillin,
Kansas City is where his heart's still in,
A town where Blue Cross
Pays for barbecue sauce
As a drug along with penicillin.

My hero Stephen Sondheim
Is adventurous too, just as I'm,
And rather than rhyme
Him with 4/4 time,
I'll have him dance a macarena.

It was a sleepy crowd, after cocktail hour and a big lunch, expecting a lecture on the role of the arts in bringing about social justice, a sleeper, but the scattered laughter awakened them, and S.S., the man himself, told me he loved it and I wrote his limerick out on a program. A compliment from Mr. Sondheim makes the stars stop where they are. I was happy all the way to the subway on 157th and the ride on the downtown 1 to 59th and the switch to the uptown B. I told Jenny, "Stephen Sondheim liked my limericks." "I know," she said. "I was there." I said it so it would be overheard by others in the car and I think it was though they were too cool to say, "Wow." I would never drop his name if I were in Minnesota nor should I mention it in a book, but I'm writing in New York right now so I have and I will once more. Stephen Sondheim. Me. My limericks.

Despite my awkwardness and my face like a brick wall, I am a happy man, I believe. What I've thought of as "depression" was merely disappointment, no relation to the real thing. I walk across the Washington Avenue Bridge over the Mississippi where the poet John Berryman climbed over the rail, waved goodbye, and leaped to his death in the coal yard below, and it has no reality for me, what would drive a person to the railing, let alone leap. I once spent a night in the Sun Valley Lodge, where Hemingway stayed with his mistresses before they became his third and fourth wives and where, I suppose, he imagined he had turned the corner and he thought, *At last! Someone who gets me.* The lodge is a stone's throw from the cemetery where his body lies. Doctors were charmed by his celebrity, a Nobel Prize winner, and released him from the hospital. He was 62. He went back to Idaho and put the shotgun to his head and blew his brains out. Now I'm 80. I don't understand this story whatsoever. People write about it as tragic fate and I believe every day is a new day. I'm not in denial, I'm simply ignorant, having never been down that road or anywhere close to it. I'm not from that part of town. Maybe great celebrity can cost you your close friends, the ones who would grab you before you could leap. Maybe you'd feel unworthy of the attention. But how do you give up curiosity about tomorrow? I don't get it.

Berryman jumped off the bridge at 57. Anne Sexton was 45, Sylvia Plath, 30. Virginia Woolf waded into the river at 59. I had two friends who suffered from depression, for which they had no words. To be spared it is a matter of luck. My dear Corinne paddled a canoe out onto Lake Cayuga one moonlit night in 1986, her pockets full of rocks, and overturned it and drowned. She was 43, taught economics at Wells College, and she missed out on what should've been a good life.

I'm 80 and still a stranger to genuine suffering. My grandma stood in the graveyard sobbing, her shoulders shaking, when we buried my aunt Ruth, Grandma's oldest child. My mother sobbed at my brother Philip's funeral. And I stand on stage and do a funny monologue about funerals in Lake Wobegon. That's my line of work. At Corinne's funeral, listening to a rental minister attempt to comfort us with generalities, I didn't go forward to look at her body. I've tried to keep her alive. Missing, but around nearby and well remembered.

I once walked the wall of names at the Vietnam Memorial in Washington, looking for the name of Henry Hill, a star of Anoka High School, and thinking about my own avoidance of the draft. I got an order to report for induction and I wrote back and said I wouldn't and I didn't. I waited for the knock on the door and it never happened. I don't consider it desertion, I call it a war not worth dying in.

And so was World War I. In America, men marched off to it proudly, bands playing blazing marches before cheering crowds. The Civil War belonged to their grandfathers, they needed one of their own. They arrived in Europe too late for the battle of Verdun, which went on for most of 1916, German artillery versus French infantry, outmoded strategy versus modern technology, men in deep barricaded trenches dashing across the desolate terrain toward the guns. Three-quarters of a million died for rotten feudal empires that were themselves dying, princes festooned with feathered helmets and unearned medals, and all of it blessed by cardinals and bishops and thereby the groundwork was laid for Bolshevism and Buchenwald and World War II. It was insanity.

Europeans fled from the zeal of revolutionaries and the madness of despots to come to our shores, despite our bad food and difficult language: they wanted their kids to have an easier time of it and we do. It's a land of hopeful progress. In my father's lifetime, anti-Semitism faded—we were a Christian family and I heard no derogation of Jews, literal or implied—and in my lifetime, we went from "homosexuality" to "gay," from a shameful path to a plain adjective, like "tall" or "thirty-year-old." People are who they are. In my daughter's lifetime, racism may well become history—too many various shades for color to be an issue.

As Anne Frank wrote, "Despite everything, I still believe that people are really good at heart. ... I can feel the sufferings of millions and yet, if I look up into the heavens, I think that it will all come right, that this cruelty too will end, and that peace and tranquility will return again." If this child hiding from Nazis in an attic in 1943 could be cheerful, then by God so can I.

My first mother-in-law, Marjorie O'Blennes, rose from a hardscrabble life in North Dakota, dust blowing through the windows, her father and brother drunk in the barn, and she worked hard to create a cheerful and mannerly life in a nice home. She worked all week in a clothing warehouse and Sunday was her big day, laughing, smoking a Winston, Rob Roy in hand, the table set with her best china and crystal, lighthearted talk, no politics, no arguments, the pot roast in the oven, and if her daughter could be persuaded to sit down at the piano and play Chopin, the day achieved the elegance she craved. After dinner I washed dishes and talked about what I was writing, and the woman was completely happy, the dust didn't blow, the drunks stayed in the barn.

My parents didn't smoke or drink but they loved Sundays and adored each other and even though Hitler had overrun much of Europe and people could see what was coming, nonetheless those two nestled in each other's arms and took their pleasure and I appeared nine months and fifteen minutes after the bombing of Pearl Harbor, living proof of enthusiastic cheerfulness in the face of tragedy.

8

The Plateau

Becoming 80 is a boon and a blessing to a man who spent his middle age in a fever of activity, like a wasp trying to fly through a window screen. I accepted all invitations, lecture tours, orchestra concerts, the Saturday show, the daily *Writer's Almanac,* book contracts, newspaper columns—I did everything except weddings, baptisms, and funerals. Eighty came as a huge relief: it was a plateau from which you look back and see your life in perspective, a great luxury, to observe the calamitous confusions of ambition, the hundreds of airport terminals and backstages, the auditoriums where I listened to an unctuous introduction like Karo syrup poured on Wonder Bread and realized he was talking about Me, the holidays when leisure was misery, the misbegotten romances (*What did I see in her? I was pleased by what she seemed to see in me.),* the sale of that house

I loved on Goodrich Avenue with the screened front porch. But also the impulsive moves that turned out well, like the dozen ocean cruises and all the music and dancing and outright fun, and the video essay I once did for CBS-TV, which was covering the NCAA basketball tournament that year, which I concluded by tossing a ball over my right shoulder, without looking, and hitting a swisher from the free-throw line, which impressed a number of people. And the expensive trip, New York to Southampton, aboard the *Queen Mary 2,* to celebrate my turning 70, and for ten years now, I have put myself to sleep at night by standing at the rail as the ship slips across New York Harbor past Miss Liberty and under the Verrazano Bridge and out to sea toward England. Thousands of nights of sleep for the purchase of an ocean passage. A bargain.

I grew up Sanctified Brethren and listened to preachers talk about the imminence of death, an iceberg waiting to sink our ship—so how did I get into the comedy trade? Fundamentalism is not fun, just as California is not about cauliflower nor Virginia about virginity. Occasionally I hear someone use the word "beseech" or "vouchsafe" or "propitiation" and I know I'm in the company of another evangelical and I want to throw my arms around him and commiserate. We never sang up-tempo, only dirges. Women kept silent in church because the sound of their voices would lead men to think impure thoughts. We didn't dance because it could lead to fornication. My family sat around the dinner table and said very little because we were evangelicals and believed that every word that comes out of your mouth should be to the glory of the Lord, which is a very high standard indeed so we sat in silence wondering what God wanted us to say. Surely not jokes. But I got a taste of comedy at dinner when Dad thanked God for His goodness and mercy and the death of our Savior, I put a couple peas on my spoon or a pat of potato and flipped it at my good sister whose eyes were closed during prayer, and after the Amen she found food on herself and she glared at me accusingly but Mother never reprimanded me and surely that was because she'd done something similar in her childhood. Comedy and reverence are not incompatible. Reverence bestows the liberty to be playful. We are not guilty criminals awaiting the gallows, we are children of God, our Creator loves us, and with joy in our hearts we flip peas at the righteous.

We spent a good deal of time, perhaps too much, in the Book of Revelation with the Tribulation, the pit of scorpions, the sea turning to blood, the Antichrist, Armageddon, people in such pain that they chewed their tongues off, and then of course the Judgment, but Scripture also says, "Seek and ye shall find, knock and it shall be opened unto you," and what you find, whether you seek it or not, is that when you grow up in a dark religious cult, once you're freed from it you become very very happy.

Pure unadulterated blind luck is my secret, which is not the same thing as privilege. Privilege is having a chauffeur and luck is when the train arrives just as you come through the turnstile and it stops, doors open, and you board without missing a step and now your entire day up to that point feels perfectly timed, and you feel blessed. Having a chauffeur just makes you feel sheepish.

Good luck: ten years old, playing softball, I dropped an easy pop-up on the playground—looked up—there it was—then it bounced off my forehead, and kids laughed and jeered, especially the Durbins, the bullies of the school, three skinny boys, mouth-breathers with small feral eyes who liked to jump a kid and knock him down and punch the cookies out of him. I passed their house every morning on my way to school and their dog chased me and they yelled at me all the terrible things they planned to do, and I dreaded them. I asked Mrs. Moehlenbrock to let me spend recess in the school library and she said yes and it changed my life. I read like crazy that year, read *Black Beauty, Little Britches, A Christmas Carol, The Three Musketeers, Penrod, Huckleberry Finn, Kidnapped, Robinson Crusoe, Dr. Jekyll and Mr. Hyde,* and *Pilgrim's Progress,* one after the other. I fell behind in math, didn't understand multiplicity or divisiveness or fractionalism, but she told me I was her brightest pupil and it lit up my life.

Had I caught the ball, I might've become a popular boy, succeeded in college and gone to law school, an articulate self-assured man, gotten elected to the Senate, run for president as a Republican in 2000 and beaten Al Gore but in the flush of success I would've not noticed the ticking time bomb of my mitral valve and would've collapsed on the hustings, a tall man falling, clutching his chest, making a quacking sound—and instead of that, thanks to the dropped ball, I become this reclusive guy on the radio who spends his twilight years enjoying his good fortune.

From the dropped pop-up on, instead of competing with my peers as a smart child would, I sought the approval of teachers and elders. I was a kid trying to impersonate a man of 45. Other kids called me "Professor." I had no desire to be Most Popular Boy, I wanted to be Class Genius. I joined no teams, no clubs, I was a loner. I sat in the lunchroom with other loners. I enjoyed hoeing corn and mowing the lawn, working in straight lines, which naturally leads to writing, and weeding is a form of editing, so I gravitated to a nest under the stairs where I read books and did some writing in a spiral notebook. Other kids joined 4-H where, working side by side with others, you learned cooperation and how to get along in a group and gained valuable social skills. I did not. I was briefly a Boy Scout but the uniform was embarrassing since I had no merit badges on mine and other boys did as they rose through the ranks. I did not rise. Thanks to separatist Brethren teaching, being a loner felt righteous. I became the only boy in my school who wrote poetry. The Durbins didn't know poetry from pottery. I wrote:

Let me remember this October day.
Night falls, the moon appears, the Milky Way.
The butterfly knows he will die
In a day, or an hour,
But lands on the flower,
Inserts his connector
And drinks the nectar.
I eat a golden apple and
Sit in the grass, my dog's nose in my hand.

I was a reader who kept trying my hand at writing, hoping something would come of it eventually, and was mostly oblivious to the opinions of others. My mother talked to her sister Elsie every day, it was her lifeline; my confidants were dead authors. I was dedicated to writing, one thing I could do without asking for help. My father built the house I grew up in, dug the basement, poured concrete, raised the walls, did the plumbing, planted a lawn and garden, and I could've learned a lot from him but I did not pay attention; he was a giant of competence and I was fearful of making a mistake so I absented myself. My brother Philip watched closely and became an engineer. I was my mother's son—she who loved Fibber McGee and his wife, Molly, of 79 Wistful Vista and their neighbor Throckmorton P. Gildersleeve and Wallace Wimple. She turned up the radio and laughed at all the stock punchlines. I enjoyed hearing my mother laugh, she who worked so hard making a life for her family—I don't know anybody who worked harder than Grace Keillor—and it was a beautiful thing to hear her laugh.

That summer I turned 11, my Grandpa Denham died and I was allowed to attend the funeral. My only previous encounter with death was staring at the Egyptian mummy in the Minneapolis Public Library. His funeral, seeing the tears of my aunts, the stolid faces of his sons George and Jim and Bill, was a high point amid the crushing boredom of that summer, mostly spent sitting on the riverbank, hurling rocks at sticks floating along, too old to play cowboys, too young for softball. That summer my mother made my dad take me with him when he drove a car to New York as a favor to a neighbor whose husband was an Army captain stationed in Germany and had arranged for it to be shipped to him. Dad had been stationed in New York during the war and still had friends there. Mother didn't think the father of six children should be gallivanting around alone in Manhattan, so off we went, I was his ball and chain.

It was the trip of all trips—the two-lane highways through Indiana and Ohio, the country inn in Pennsylvania with the high poster bed, Valley Forge, the whine of traffic in the Lincoln Tunnel, the towers of Manhattan silvery in the afternoon sun, streets jammed with pushcart peddlers shouting in strange languages. I was knocked out by New York. And I had my father all to myself for two weeks for the one and only time in my life. Once in Times Square I wandered away from him and it scared him, the thought that I might get lost, and he ran and grabbed my hand, and I remember this—knowing that my dad loved me. He'd never say it, of course, but he did.

Dad told me he had been an Army postal clerk and people on the street looked at his uniform and treated him like a hero and restaurants served him dinner, no charge, and theaters let him in for free. He admitted this freely, though Brethren were supposed to shun theaters—the Lord was sufficient for us, we didn't need chorus girls and razzmatazz. A great discovery for me, that my father had broken a rule and also that some people had died in battle and others had had a wonderful time in uniform. But the real discovery was when I came home, that I was the only student in Benson School who'd seen New York. The one and only.

It was a gigantic rise in stature. I'd been bullied at school before—kids'd hold the chair for me to sit down on and then pull it away so I crashed to the floor with macaroni and cheese all over me. They'd tie my shoelaces together. They'd throw water at me so it looked like I wet my pants. Gave me the cruel nickname "Foxfart." But no more. Now I was the sixth-grade sophisticate who stood up in front of the school and talked about the Bronx and the Battery, the people riding in a hole in the ground, Coney Island and the waves of the Atlantic crashing in and going to see the Dodgers and standing on the 86th floor of the Empire State. I felt the advantage of having good material. *Were you scared?* they asked. *Did you see criminals? Were there a lot of Negroes?* "Yes," I said. "There were Negroes and I talked to them and they talked to me." The Durbins accused me of lying but nobody listened to them and they slunk away in defeat. I told about the heat wave in New York when Dad and I slept on a fire escape six stories up and one night we spread a sheet in a park and slept on the grass along with hundreds of others.

"Weren't you scared?"

"No, I was asleep."

"How could you sleep with all those people you didn't even know?"

"I felt safe with them around. I just closed my eyes and went to sleep."

Around the time I came back from New York, my great-uncle Llewellyn—we called him Uncle Lew—began visiting our house on Saturday nights, bringing a box of sugar wafers and a bag of peanut brittle. He owned the Ada Claire Candy Company, named for his wife, a plump lady, quite bejeweled, with numerous jangly bracelets on her wrists, who spoke not a word all evening, as Lew talked about his grandfather, my great-great-grandfather, David Powell, and I lay silent and still on the floor at his feet.

David's father-in-law, William Cox, was a British seaman aboard a British warship who suffered miserably as all lowly seamen did, living in dank quarters below decks, fed garbage, whipped with a cat-o'-nine-tails for minor infractions, and when the first mate yelled "All hands aloft!" the seamen scrambled up the rigging even in a storm lest they be stripped naked and whipped for insubordination.

But one day in harbor in Charleston, South Carolina, William was fastening rat guards to the lines holding the ship to dock when the second mate's attention was diverted by a fine young woman with a parasol approaching the gangway to visit the captain, and William saw his chance and slipped up the street past tobacco and sugar warehouses and broke into a run, knowing that if caught he'd go straight to the gallows. He hopped aboard a horse-drawn wagon train and buried himself in a load of potatoes and was suddenly free of his old life.

He escaped detection, made his way to Pennsylvania, and met Elizabeth Emily Boggs and married her. His daughter Martha Ann married David Powell, a Pennsylvania farmer, a restless man who felt the pull of the golden West, and every few years, though he had good crops of oats and corn and timothy, he sold his farm and packed the babies in the wagon, a milk cow tied to the tailgate, and migrated westward, Ohio, Michigan, Illinois, Iowa, while bearing eight children, three others died and were buried along the way.

It was a saga of enterprise and independence, putting misery behind you and reaching for a brighter tomorrow, very different from the dutiful Denhams and cautious Keillors, who accepted hardship as the Lord's Will and awaited deliverance by the Rapture.

In 1859 David left his family in the care of his three eldest sons and headed for Colorado and the gold rush, passed through Cheyenne territory and traded with them, hunted antelope to feed his party, tried to cross the Missouri at flood tide, eight wagons lashed together but his wagon tipped over and a bag of sugar fell overboard and turned to molasses. He wrote Martha Ann, "Hard rain & wind storm. Cattle stampede & we had to be on horseback all night. Awful night. Men all tired and want to leave. Horses all gave out & men refused to do anything. Wet all night. Worked all day hard in the river trying to make the cattle swim & did not get one over.

Had to turn back sick and discouraged. Have not got the blues but am in a Hell of a fix."

I adored this story, I whispered the words "hell of a fix" to myself. David got to Denver, found no gold claims available, served a term in the territorial legislature, returned to Iowa and Martha Ann who had waited four years for him. He begged her to come west with him and she put her foot down. He tried to charm her into heading west and a few months later she was pregnant with her twelfth child, Edgar Alonzo. In 1864 they went west to Missouri. She dispatched her older boys, including my great-grandfather James Wesley Powell, to head east and collect the remains of the three children who had died en route and bring them back for burial in Missouri. And then David got it in his head to settle in Oklahoma. He made a claim near Hennessey, built a house and stable, dug a well, and one day he sat down under a tree, leaned against it, and died of a heart attack, an extraordinary ancestor, a farmer who'd kept on the move his whole life.

His granddaughters were my grandmother Dora and her twin sister, Della, who came north to Minnesota and became the first female railroad telegraphers in the U.S., identical twins who operated as one, sharing the same uniform, in Anoka. They had learned Morse code so they could give each other answers to questions in class. Dora took up teaching at a country school and at the end of the term, the farmer from across the road (he was on the school board) came over to help clean the blackboards and then he tried to kiss her. She said, "I ran away but not so fast that he couldn't catch me if he tried." Which he did, and so the deal was sealed. She liked him because she could hear him singing in the fields as he plowed or mowed hay; he had a lovely tenor voice. And he had a mind for memorization and liked to quote poetry at length. That evening, he hitched up the horses and they drove to town and were married and returned home. He was twenty years older than she but he carried her into the house and up the stairs, leaving the horses hitched to the wagon, the reins hanging on the ground. He was not a good farmer but he was a cheerful man and they raised seven children.

I loved these stories dearly, William Cox jumping ship and David Powell pursuing a dream though a farmer and the father of a big family who named his fifth child Isaac Newton and his sixth Harriet Beecher. A man of large aspirations. There was no Scripture message whatsoever in the stories, only the lesson that you should follow your heart, take to the road, find your fortune or not but not be bound by propriety.

This story was told as I lay perfectly still on the floor, hanging on every word. Always on Saturday night. Sometimes Aunt Ruth was there, correcting Uncle Lew, arguing about the details. I had many questions but dared not interrupt and now it's too late. My last aunt, Eleanor, died in 1996, and I grieve for the lost knowledge that she took with her. Except for Lew, my uncles didn't tell stories. They talked about cars and work and plumbing and of course about Scripture but never reminisced. They claimed to know nothing about family history. I was dumbfounded: how could you live your life and not remember it. Of course they remembered, but they were leery of venturing into those precincts of the past. I believe they were afraid of the feelings it might arouse.

Aunt Ina told how she'd gone to a car dealer in Minneapolis in 1928 and though she'd never driven a car, she bought one and she and two girlfriends drove on country roads all the way to Yellowstone Park to see the geysers and then sold the car and took the train back to Minnesota to resume a circumspect life. Aunt Ruth told how Grandpa woke his children on a winter night and bundled them up and took them into the woods to see a silver timber wolf who was baying at the moon. Aunt Jo told about sitting in the schoolhouse doing her math problems and a girl said, "Look, your house is on fire" and Jo looked and it was. Mother said that when she was 13, she and Elsie were doing dishes in the kitchen on Longfellow and they got to laughing so hard that Mother knocked two of her sister Ruby's pies off the windowsill where they were cooling—she said, "And that was when I learned how to bake a pie, two of them, in half an hour."

The stories I cherished were the ones with no clear moral: the sailor jumping ship, the wayfaring farmer, Dora and Della using Morse code to share answers in class.

And now I'm older than Lew was and I buy peanut brittle to remind me of those Saturday nights, the quavery voice of the storyteller, me lying on the floor, my face next to his black leather high-top shoes, not moving a muscle for fear the story would stop and I would miss the messages from the past. Even as a child, I knew my family believed in keeping secrets secret. They were not gossips. The scandal of my parents' marriage was tightly guarded by dozens of witnesses for seventy years. An aunt had been abandoned by her husband who ran off with a schoolteacher, leaving three children behind. I asked my mother about it and she would say just so much and no more. I heard whispers about a Brethren man who was teasing his sister's fiancé about shotgun weddings and he grabbed a shotgun, not knowing it was loaded, and pulled the trigger and killed his future brother-in-law. He was the father of an aunt who married into the family. I knew these people. I could've asked but the darkness was so deep, I feared I could be banished for asking.

I still want to know this story and I know it's too late. I believe it is not a story about evil but about forgiveness and a decision made secretly and simultaneously by dozens of people to put the matter behind them and let the future be cheerful. I admire people who can do that. I need to know the story so I can honor them. I can't love someone without knowing them and walking a mile in their shoes.

My father valued stability and I had my sights set high, like the proctologist who studied the moons of Uranus. I registered at the University the month I turned 18 and I walked up the Mall from Morrill Hall and past Walter Library and there I fell in with six or seven very dark-skinned men who were jabbering in French and I didn't think, "Oh. Africa." I thought, "North Minneapolis." Their French sounded perfect. Black men coming to the U to major in French: it blew my mind. The University was to me what Colorado was to David Powell. I landed in September and a month later I had a noon newscast on the student radio station, WMMR, and the friends I found there were all Jews—Halper, Leventhal, Bernstein, Goldman, all of them smart, funny, irreverent, looking for an angle, not burdened by my "Don't think you're somebody" Protestantism, amused by my picking up Yiddishisms from them. But the idea of remaking myself took hold and I set out to be writerly and wrote for the *Ivory Tower* magazine and made a rash decision after college to quit a comfortable job and to earn my living writing fiction. Then, a mere two months later, the effusive letter from Roger Angell accepting a story of mine for *The New Yorker*, which I sat down and read over and over. The magazine paid me $500 for the story; my monthly rent was $80. I've been in favor of prosperity ever since.

Publishing in the magazine of Benchley, Thurber, Perelman, Liebling, and Salinger was a sort of knighthood, a purple sash bestowed with a sword and cape and helmet, and it gave me the repute to land my own weekly radio show, *A Prairie Home Companion*. No need to beg for foundation grants, wrangle with management, kiss the feet of wealthy patrons, I just said, "Let's do it," and we did it. Lack of talent landed me the job; my friends were musicians who could play tunes with intricate fingering at fast tempos. They didn't want to be the yahoo who says hello to the folks and tells jokes and introduces the talent, they wanted to be the talent, and so I got the job and forty years of job security. I sang the theme song and talked to small audiences that soon got bigger. It was easy. If Roger Angell had rejected the story, I'd be a school bus driver yelling at the kids to shut the hell up or a cook in a diner hearing Mabel yell "Adam and Eve on a raft" and I'd make two poached eggs on toast. But instead I put on a tux and combed my hair and I sang:

Smells so lovely when you pour it,
You will want to drink a quart
Of coffee.
It's delicious all alone, it's
Also good with doughnuts,
Black coffee.
Coffee stimulates your urges,
It is served in Lutheran churches,
Keeps the Swedes and the Germans
Awake through the sermons.
Have a pot of it today,
I'm sure you'll say it's awfully good coffee.

The audience enjoyed my doggerel, and I never wrote a serious poem after that except love sonnets to my wife. Mainly I've written limericks. The show went up on National Public Radio in 1980, NPR then being the American BBC, soon to be the Mother Church of Woke, but what I brought to it was immature humor.

There was an old man of Nantucket
Who died. He just kicked the bucket.
And when he was dead,
They found that instead
Of Nantucket he came from Woonsocket.
His billfold was right in his pocket.

Limericizing is a tricky craft like making a model ship in a bottle; people look down on it who can't write one themselves. I write a good limerick and it makes me happy all day.

I can write one for my daughter:

A young gentlewoman named Maia
Decided she must satisfy a
Powerful urge
To run into church
And cry, "Hallelujah! Hey! Hiya!"

Or one for Whitman:

Here is a yawp for old Walt,
A poet who's well worth his salt
Though sometimes he'll slip
And just let her rip
And say, "Camerados! What is this blade of grass?
Who am I?
Who are you" And you have to say, HALT.

The limerick is very precise, though of course one can take liberties and it gives an old man the freedom to be juvenile, which I cherish.

A writer I know (maybe me)
Stands at the toilet to pee.
His lover has taught him
To aim for the bottom,
Square in the middle,
And try not to piddle
Outside of the periphery.

I sit in church Sunday morning and if the homily wanders, I simply write.

Our Savior the Lord Jesus Christ
Was, for our sins, sacrificed,
Was raised from the dead
To become Living Bread,
Whole wheat, with raisins, unsliced.

Did I say it's odd for a Brethren boy to go into comedy? I take that back. Solomon was a great comedian. "The rivers run into the sea and yet the sea is not full." That's a joke. "Whoever increases knowledge increases sorrow." That was a scream at one time. And "The sun also ariseth, and the sun goeth down, and hasteth to his place where he arose."

They heard that and the pomegranates came out their noses. Solomon knew that we're all losers, that having a ton of money only makes it possible to be miserable in ways unavailable to the clerk and carpenter. As Solomon said, "The race is not to the swift nor the battle to the strong nor riches to men of understanding, but time and chance happeneth to them all." That's the meaning of comedy right there in thirty words or less. You're fast, you trip on your shoelace and fall down and the competition runs over you; you're strong and you lift the 220-pound barbell and do your squat and the sheer effort makes you shit in your shorts and drop the weight on your feet and let out a girlish shriek that goes viral on YouTube; you're smart and get a confidential tip and invest all your money in Balkonian bonds and then discover that Balkonia is a fictional country. It's Friday, your bank is closed; you call Monday morning and find out the check was cashed, you're broke. The joke's on you, hot shot.

But none of that happened to me. Instead, I went to lunch with the sister of a friend of my younger sister and we launched into conversation and the string section started playing and we saw a lot of each other for a while and eventually saw all of each other and we knelt in the chapel and a few years later our daughter arrived in the world at a hospital overlooking the East River in New York. I held her in my hands, a six-pounder, arms and legs waving, bright dark eyes.

At the age of two months, she got a laughing fit at seeing a box with a spring lid that snapped shut with a loud whap. We brought her to Minnesota and my parents and elderly aunts and uncles passed her around, taking turns holding her for a few minutes, maybe the last infant they would hold in this life, then handing her to the next one. She loved nursery school when she was two and Seth and Mai-Britt took her in hand and the kids spent the day outdoors with goats and a horse and a llama. She was joyful at the sight of food and when I carried her on my shoulders and twirled her around she whooped with delight. She adored dogs. She lived entirely in the present. She soon figured out that Mom was the boss, Dad was an easy touch. Once she wrote *Daddy* in enormous letters in green chalk on the driveway and for weeks, despite the rain, it was there every morning when I backed the car out of the garage.

I took her to the State Fair and toted her through the livestock barns where she touched a newly shorn sheep. We slid down the Giant Slide together on a burlap bag and she laughed all the way to the bottom. She ate part of a corn dog that I pre-chewed for her and had honey ice cream at the Horticulture building. After her tonsillectomy, in a half-stupor, she saw me—I who had gently but forcefully put the mask over her face so she could be anesthetized—and she stuck out her tongue with real conviction.

I saw her clearly one afternoon when she was six, swinging on the neighbor's rope swing, laughing and laughing, and on the backswing her head disappeared into the branches of the apple tree, she found the point where joy and fear meet, where religion begins, as her head went up into the blossoms, and then she put her feet down and skidded to a stop and toppled over in the grass, still laughing. And saw me and ran to me and put her arms around me. "I love you so much," she said. I have on my phone a video of her on a water ride looking at me and seeing my pants are wet and laughing hysterically. The day we dropped her at boarding school was an agonizing day, walking away from a weeping child in the arms of a teacher, and driving down the road telling each other we were doing the right thing and not believing it. She didn't change her clothes for four days because her mother had hugged her in those clothes and she wanted to remember. But she did well with schedules and assignments and graduated in 2019 and at the dance in the gym I got teary-eyed dancing with her to "Wonderful World" and singing to her, "I hear babies cry, I watch them grow; they'll learn much more than I'll ever know." Which is true in her case. And the next day the Class stood on the green grass and on the count of three, they flung their mortarboards in the air and hers flew higher than anyone else's. Now she's 25, a social butterfly, happy in a scrum of friends. She inherited this from her mother. I call her and she answers and I hear chatter in the background and she says, "Could I call you back later?" So I know where I stand in her world: important but not crucial. I'm happy for her. Somehow she was born with a lightheartedness I had to work hard to find. "Make me laugh," she says, and I give her the razzberry and she laughs. I expected to get a brilliant neurotic self-loathing daughter who can't seem to find herself and instead we got Maia.

9

Purpose ·

Two weeks after my 80th, I went in for heart surgery at Mayo, a procedure I was looking forward to, the surgeon having said we had a 98.2 percent chance of success, which, at 80, seems golden. We weren't out to curtail some malign wasting disease but to replace the mitral valve, like putting in a new carburetor. Jenny held my hand as I was prepped for surgery and they wheeled me into the chilly OR and laid me out on the table surrounded by young women and men in blue scrubs and the anesthesiologist put a hand on my shoulder and leaned down and whispered, "I'm going to take good care of you" and a minute later I was back in a hospital room and a nurse said, "We're going to slide you onto your bed, my friend," and they did, and a moment later, she said, "I'm going to have a look at your groin, my friend." The wire they run up to your heart to change the arrhythmia goes up a vein in your groin. So she checked and the wound looked good. She pulled the sheet back up. She brushed the hair out of my eyes. I was dazzled by her kindness. She asked if I felt any pain. No, not a bit. She made friendly small talk while checking tubes, asked me to squeeze her hands, wiggle my fingers, look into a bright light, push up against her hand pulling my foot down, smile, raise my eyebrows, follow her finger with my eyes, and when I did, she said, "Awesome," "Fantastic," "Excellent." She brought me a small plastic container of applesauce, the Monet *Garden at Giverny* of applesauce, Chopin's applesauce étude "La Tristesse," sauce from the apple Eve gave to Adam, the applesauce of knowledge, and I thank God for it.

The surgeon said, "When we opened you up and looked around, we could see you're eighty, but the valve should be good for another fifteen years, maybe more." Two cardiologists listened to it and said there was no more squooshing, just a good steady beat. I walked the halls of St. Mary's hospital with an elegant black cane that had belonged to my mother and I was flying high, clicking the cane on the marble floor, planning to write the book you are reading now. For me, writing a book about cheerfulness is like writing about ski-jumping, a venture into new territory. I went through decades of busy striving and confusion and dissatisfaction and now I felt secure in my skis, looking down the steep chute, knees bent, leaning forward, pushing off.

I was glad to postpone my demise and get fifteen more years though I know that longevity is not a great blessing for the younger generation. Nature has no interest in our twilight years, it only wanted us to beget, to raise the offspring, then set them free, and get out of their way. God created erectile dysfunction because old men can't be trusted to raise little kids. It's nature's way of saying, *Enough out of you.*

Past 70, you become an obstruction, a drain on the economy, a waste of good shelf space. Back in my youth, when old people could no longer climb stairs, off to Happy Acres they went and died of boredom in their 70s. Now, thanks to modern medicine and Medicare, they may live into their 90s, dozing on a Florida patio and conversing with a margarita. Schools are cutting back on music and drama so the state can pay for Gramps to get an MRI when he has a headache and thus the kids don't get exposed to Mozart or Shakespeare. But if an old lady's bowels get backed up, they'll hook her up to a high-frequency colonizer and vibrate the poop out of her and charge the government $1,252.78 for the experience, meanwhile they give Viagra to men in nursing homes to keep them from rolling out of bed at night. People who once were useful—engineers, doctors, botanists, theologians—retire at 65 and take up the hobby lifestyle and go to the Grand Canyon and take pictures of it and are thrilled to be artists. The world doesn't need more pictures of the Grand Canyon. There are enough pictures of the Grand Canyon to fill the Grand Canyon.

A person needs to feel useful. Honors and titles mean very little: there are thousands of ordinary folks in town who do more actual good than the Vice President for Impact & Influence. Like the teacher I saw at a grade school choir concert who sat, as the kids sang for the parents and grandparents who clapped and cheered, and she held on her lap a little girl who had a slight disorder that made her terribly sensitive to sound and who wore a pair of ear pads as the teacher stroked her back and jiggled her gently. Rather than shut the child up in a quiet classroom, she comforted her and let her be part of the deal. It wasn't her job to do that, she just saw the problem and took the child in her arms.

So I have to find my own way to be useful to justify the expense of my medical care. So, following the August surgery, I did a *Prairie Home Companion* show in October, another in November, a third in December, out of obligation to Dr. Dearani and his surgical team who'd worked for six hours to replace my fluttery 80-year-old mitral valve with one from a young pig. It's my duty to make their work mean something. Mary Oliver wrote, "Tell me, what is it you plan to do with your one wild and precious life?" I'm starting a new career as an octogenarian stand-up working theaters in Mid-America and the South, doing comedy, poetry, history, and knowing that most of the crowd is Republican, I lead them in a cappella song starting with "America" and on to doo-wop and "How Great Thou Art" and the audience is moved by the beauty of their own harmonies, lefties and Trumpists together. And then the quiet week in Lake Wobegon. And when that's done I will be a family historian, ready to tell Gen Z about Thomas Keillor's voyage from Yorkshire in 1774 and the Crandalls who supported the King and had to flee the Revolution and William Cox who escaped hanging and David Powell the migrating farmer and Grandpa who kissed Dora Powell and married her and carried her upstairs without unhitching the horses.

Fear of death is not a good enough reason to go on living: you need a higher purpose than just respiration. My mother lived to be 97, which gave me time to try to make up for the grief I'd caused her. And she got to meet her last grandchild, my daughter. And I got to tell stories about her on the radio, knowing she was listening, stories in which she was a sharpshooter in a Wild West Show, shooting the cigar out of the ringmaster's hand as she galloped, blindfolded, past. She enjoyed it though she did remind me that the story was not true.

I intend to be a cheerful old man and show the young that such is possible: with a measure of luck, life can become more and more enjoyable. My mother, on many a Sunday morning as we left for church, wondered if she had left the iron on but we never turned around and drove back to check. She also imagined one of us might put our tongue on an iron railing in January and the tongue freezes to it and firemen come and yank you loose. But we went outdoors anyway and we never licked an iron railing though of course we considered it. She shed these anxieties in her old age. When she was 94 I put her on a plane to London where she'd take a train up to Scotland, and she was giddy as a teenager.

I started out hoping to be a brilliant writer and then I hoped to earn money from writing, and now I just want to be useful. I saw one of my novels at a yard sale with rust-colored rings on the cover: it had been used as a coaster. I intended it to be an intellectual experience but at least it had protected furniture from water damage. So I'm a writer of coasters. So Debussy puts me to sleep. Everything has a purpose. And coasters can also be shims, to steady a shaky table or chair.

Simple usefulness can lead to great things unintended

by the maker: Edison worked to design a machine for managers to dictate letters into and it took another direction—Caruso sang into it and Jimmie Rodgers and King Oliver and the recording business burst forth into the 20th century and the hybrid genius of America bloomed and blew the seeds of jazz and blues and rock 'n' roll around the world. You never know. Brilliant minds at MIT and UCLA and the Rand Corporation created the interconnection of giant computers to enable scattered communities of scholars to share data and it became the internet, which enables you to transmit photographs of your dogs Lulu and Gimpy or disseminate angry blogs excoriating your enemies or look at varieties of pornography you never knew existed. The jury is still deliberating this case.

10

The Sage of Concord

The pragmatist Mr. Dewey
Said of Ralph whom he knew, "He
'S not transcendental,
Just sentimental,
Not based on science,
Not one of the giants.
As for 'Self-Reliance,' ptui."

I spent a week after the procedure at St. Mary's Hospital and it occurred to me that "procedure" is not a good word to describe something that gives you more time in this world. "Procedure" is good enough for clearing a paper jam in a printer, but what was done for me was miraculous. Thanks to scientific wizardry, I was now, in effect, walking on water.

I brought Ralph Waldo Emerson with me, a book of his essays that Uncle Lew had left to me, which his son Henry had neglected to send but his son Russell forwarded it with a note of apology. It was an 1841 edition with David Powell's name on the front page, in an elegant hand with a fancy D and P. "Grandpa wanted you to have this but was afraid of offending your father who looked on Emerson as an unbeliever, but you are old enough to decide about that yourself," wrote Russell, whom I'd never met. The package was postmarked in Bend, Oregon.

Back in my English major years, I had dismissed Emerson as a manufacturer of maxims ("To be great is to be misunderstood.") of the sort you could make into wall plaques ("When it is dark enough, you can see the stars.") and as Emerson himself said, "I hate quotations. Tell me what you know." With Thoreau's *Walden* and *A Week on the Concord and Merrimack Rivers*, I had a sense of a man behind the words, but Emerson felt like a long avenue with billboards every hundred feet ("A foolish consistency is the hobgoblin of little minds.") and back then at the U, I put him on the shelf and forgot about him.

Henry Thoreau, in comparison, was something of a crank and a fraud. He advocated civil disobedience, spent a day in jail, and Emerson paid his fine. When Henry said, "The mass of men lead lives of quiet desperation," he may have been thinking about himself. He usually did. What he knew about the mass of men was a good deal less than what he knew about squirrels. I was impressed by him in college and then never picked him up again.

The great transcendental Thoreau
Went to live in the woods long ago
And wrote lovely prose
While his mom washed his clothes
And fixed him hot lunches to go.

Emerson, on the other hand, was a great intellect of the 19th century, a transcendentalist (whatever that may mean), a tireless lecturer, an abolitionist, and all his stuff about individualism was perfectly okay but when I was 21 I found the preachy tone tedious ("It is not the length of life but the depth," blah blah blah) and now, at the age of 80, recovering from surgery, grateful for heart repair, he became a personal friend. Especially knowing that my ancestor had held this book in his hand.

Uncle Lew remembered that David was known for reading as he worked, cultivating his fields with the reins in his right hand, a book in his left. A cultivated man, in other words. And the book of Emerson appeared well-read. So I gave him another chance. If a farmer driving horses could absorb this stuff, there must be something to it.

I discovered that Emerson can be funny ("The louder he talked of his honor, the faster we counted our spoons.") and even funnier ("There was never a child so lovely but his mother was glad to get him to sleep.") and funnier yet ("I dream of a better tomorrow, where chickens can cross the road and not be questioned about their motives."). The stuff about nonconformity and making your dreams come true, however, reminds me of some flummery I saw on Facebook last week ("Find out who you are and be that person and live that truth and everything else will come."). We are contradictions is who we are, every savant contains an idiot and on one hand he can solve six solid geometry problems in his head simultaneously and on the other hand he buys an 800-pound anvil because it's so cheap, $300, but he doesn't want his wife to know so he keeps it up in a tree in the backyard and one day he walks out back and the anvil falls on him, smooshes him flat as a pancake and he's buried in a Steinway piano case and everybody in the church thinks, "What in the name of heaven was he thinking?"

I have thought this about myself on numerous occasions, but now I need to get things under control and I read Emerson with new eyes. I see *In skating over thin ice, our safety is in our speed* and I know that the great man was also a skater. And I see *The man is the head of the house but the woman is the neck that turns the head* and I know that he was a husband. His sentences land like knuckles on an oak door. *How much of human life is lost in waiting. Hitch your wagon to a star. Go where there is no path and leave a trail. The mind, once stretched by a new idea, never returns to its original dimensions. So let us take our bloated nothingness out of the path of the divine circuits. The world we live in is but thickened light; it is all gates, all opportunities. There is no end in nature, but every end is a beginning; that there is always another dawn risen on midnoon, and under every deep a lower deep opens. Wherever snow falls, or water flows, or birds fly, wherever day and night meet in twilight, wherever is danger, and awe, and love, there is Beauty, plenteous as rain.*

The man is writing in an era of drudgery when young people languished in the cotton mills and thousands of New England men ran away to sea to escape the hopelessness of farming on poor soil and stood aboard a ship in heavy seas and hacked the blubber off the whales as they were hauled up and threw it in an oven to cook down, the deck slippery with oil, blades honed razor sharp, men sliding around as the ship pitched and rolled, and here is Emerson telling them to hitch their wagon to a star. I would've told them to hitch a rope to their belts lest they fall overboard and be eaten by sharks.

I am not so enthusiastic about individualism. His advice is all very elevated and hopeful (*Trust instinct to the end, even though you can give no reason. No law can be sacred to me but that of my nature. Do not be too squeamish or timid about your actions.*), but it seems meant for a guy with a trust fund and a staff to manage the business or at the very least a devoted wife to raise the kids and do the taxes. "Trust instinct" and "do not be too squeamish or timid" makes me think of a former president who tried to overthrow the government. As for *When a man is defeated he has a chance to learn something*, what I learned from my defeats was that I'm capable of abysmal stupidity but I already knew that. And I skip over the stuff about being uplifted by nature. I was a camp counselor one summer and spent weeks in the woods eating charred food in a cloud of insects, some of which carry dreadful diseases, and sleeping on stony ground, feeling the pangs of constipation, thinking about snakes and bears and tall trees that fall for no reason in the middle of the night. Only two great novels involve camping, *Grapes of Wrath* and *Red Badge of Courage*, and in neither book is camping done for pleasure. Camping is about boredom; it's a refugee experience. Shakespeare did not write, *When in disgrace with fortune and men's eyes, I all alone beweep my outcast state, and pitch a tent beneath the summer skies and look up at the trees and contemplate.* No, when he was in disgrace with fortune, he took comfort in remembering a woman's love. Thoreau was the great camper because no woman loved him except his mother. When I first met my wife, I noticed that she wasn't wearing hiking boots and didn't have a lanyard around her neck and didn't smell of insect repellent. It was a good start to a fine romance.

But you sit down and read Emerson and suddenly in comes a lightning stroke of a sentence—*Life is short, but there is always time enough for courtesy. Manners are the happy ways of doing things, a rich varnish, with which the routine of life is washed, and its details adorned.* You could hang your hat on that line. *There is always time enough for courtesy.* What struck me, an old man in the hospital with a Frankensteinian scar on my chest, was his insistence on cheerfulness, looking forward, seizing the day. He said exactly what was on my mind as I went through rehab, walking the treadmill, pedaling the stationary bike, lifting weights, doing my stretches. I had hated exercising but now, as Emerson said, was the beginning of something new.

Finish every day and be done with it. You have done what you could; some blunders and absurdities no doubt crept in; forget them as soon as you can. Tomorrow is a new day; you shall begin it well and serenely, and with too high a spirit to be cumbered with your old nonsense. This day, for all that, is good and fair. It is too dear, with its hopes and invitations, to waste a moment on the rotten yesterdays. Write it on your heart that every day is the best day in the year and this time, like all times, is a very good one, if we but know what to do with it.

And then, a great surprise: a note on onionskin paper

dried up by age, addressed to "Mr. Powell, Esq." from the author:

I have read your letter repeatedly and find sentiments in the lines that are solid and born of conviction and not the conventions of the day. You are fortunate to have escaped Harvard and Yale and the doubts they instill and to gather your thoughts as you harvest the bounty of your plot of ground. I have no admonitions to offer, having seldom traveled so far as Ohio, but to your Colorado aspirations I say Bravo and Godspeed. Let your private heart be guide and companion. I would sign this book to you but then the value is in the signature, not in the light of the words within, and please know that if you take the book on your westward journey, then I am a fellow traveler and am honored to be such. I admit I envy the spontaneity of your enthusiasm as I trudge from station to station, giving the same lecture to the inevitable admiring crowds; I feel I am planting beans while you are harvesting life itself. Take good care, my friend, and I trust I shall hear from you again in due course. Kind regards, R.W.E.

I sent the letter to Russell and said that it was worth money and should belong to him, that the book itself was worth a great deal to me, and he wrote back and thanked me, and I believe it was auctioned off but I don't know where it is today and I don't care. I do know that Russell and his ex-wife reconciled and left Oregon for Cape Cod and bought a fine house in Nantucket and I'm glad the letter did them good.

Cheerfulness is a choice: that's what I get from Emerson. *A man is relieved and gay when he has put his heart into his work and done his best; but what he has said or done otherwise, shall give him no peace.* So take time to know your own heart. Nobody is born smart but don't spit into the wind and don't cut the branch you're standing on because there's no feast for the miser. What I get from Whitman is breathless enthusiasm for no apparent reason, what I get from Emily Dickinson is the feeling that maybe she should take a break from embroidery and go swimming naked in the Mill River. Emerson was practical. He said to swing your legs out of bed, pull on your trousers, forget the yesterday that you wasted worrying about today, and make this day your own. Pacify your heart, put away the hucksters, agitators, the artisanal ice salesmen, so you can hear the quiet reminders of your heart. Calm yourself. Yes, you feel isolated in this sleeping city, adrift, unengaged, and wish for someone to drink coffee with whom you can trust, whom you can ask, "Do I smell bad? Is it my hair? My gloomy face? Why does the world turn away?" but this is a swamp and today is a blessed gift and now, as the sun comes up, is the time to claim it for your own. The angry man drinks his own poison so put that away and set your mind on the beautiful, a gladiolus plant in a pot, a photograph of streetlight and white house on a winter night, your lover who sleeps in the next room: when she rises in a few hours, open your arms. Put the newspaper aside for now. Don't fight with mendacity and hypocrisy, you wind up with slime all over you. Save your battles for another time: morning belongs to you.

The best cure for a bad day is to go to bed early and start over in the morning. Do your contrition as you fall asleep and when you wake up, consider yourself forgiven. Get up on the right side of the bed, set your dial toward high-spirited and hopeful, rather than the rerun of old sad movies. "Lord, don't let me be a jerk today, make me decent at least. I have disappointed enough people, I don't care to add to the total. Today, whomever I encounter, I will leave them slightly better off than before. I will ignore rudeness and be grateful for kindness. I will not think less of persons wearing Yankees caps or goth tattoos or flag pins or people who open their mouths and out comes a stream of graffiti. Each one has a spark of the divine and someday we will see this clearly."

Six a.m. and the city is only faintly lit. My early jobs as a dishwasher and parking lot attendant began at 6 a.m. and I respect this hour. It was never a bad day that had a good morning. I get up and am grateful for the sensor that switches on the light in the hallway and all is made clear, the sink and mirror, the shower, the toilet, my target below, and I let fly. And I think, "Lead, kindly light, amid the encircling gloom, lead thou me on."

I worry about the country but it's not mine to worry about, it belongs to younger people, a big boisterous republic with not so much in common these days, or so it appears: television and pop music have splintered into dozens of niches and byways, no singers like Satchmo or Sinatra or Elvis whose voices everyone recognized. Most celebrities are famous to only a slim minority. They're followed on TikTok but nobody follows them down the street because they are so numerous. But my generation hangs onto the old songs about the spacious skies and amber waves of grain, the sweet land of liberty, the oceans white with foam, the roaming buffalo, the coming of the Lord with his terrible swift sword, the chariot swinging low as we hear the whistle blow and rise up so early in the morn—we get very happy, being in a crowd that knows the words. Once, at a show in Baltimore, at an open pavilion in the Inner Harbor, not far from where Francis Scott Key wrote the words, a couple thousand people stood and sang the national anthem with gusto, the sopranos floating up high over "O'er the land of the free and the land of the brave." Everyone knew the words and people who thought they were too cool to sing somehow got into the spirit of it. The tone-deaf sang softly. It was a sweet cheerful tribal feeling and we all felt the creaturely comfort of it.

Individualism is all well and good in its place, such as the bathroom or kitchen or the driver's seat of your car, but belonging to the pluribus is a beautiful thing whether it's at the dear old Temple Bar with our glasses raised on high or the hockey arena where we stand and shout *M-I-N-N-E-S-O-T-A* or the stadium packed with Stones fans singing *Wild wild horses couldn't drag me away.* I pray we never lose the grace that taught my heart to fear and the Red River Valley, roses loving sunshine, singing in the rain, going to Montana to throw the houlihan, and the bright golden haze in the meadow. It'll be sad if the great songs go down and old acquaintance is forgot and buried under the weeping willow and the train leaves the station with two lights on behind, one light is my heart and the other is my mind.

People can walk around in the private world of headphones listening to Etaoin Shrdlu or The Quick Brown Foxes or Eff Oh and their anthems of isolation, but isolation is the enemy. Self-consciousness hits some of us hard at an early age and makes us wary of others—me, for example, too tall, a gremlin face, a fundy upbringing that said to avoid the heathen, a writerly introspection, a sense of klutziness, a bookish formality, some pretentious speech patterns—I am not anyone's first choice for a traveling partner—but that morning radio show of mine was a great gift. I made small talk on the air and listeners called the station to talk to me and I learned about the lives of dairy farmers, farm wives, first-grade teachers, a Catholic priest, a shopkeeper, a sculptor. Margaret, a college friend who became a shrink, told me, "Psychiatry saved me from depression because I got caught up in other people's lives." I lacked the experience of friendship but I found it on the 6 a.m. radio shift. Some people find it playing in bands or orchestras. My cousin Dan found it as a rural physician. Some people find it in church or coaching sports or agitating for a noble cause, but you need to get tangled up with others and stay clear of the lonesome hitchhiker blues, the misunderstood loner and neglected child, the martyred hero. You need to make yourself useful, which is a good step toward friendship. A friend is someone whose company you enjoy and whom you don't need to impress. I got into comedy by way of loneliness. When people laugh, it's friendship.

I don't feel friendship when I'm in a crowd of Democrats; I feel I'm among people who can talk my head off about empowerment, healing, authentic belonging, and creating an anti-oppressive life-affirming environment of socioeconomic equity but they don't know how to clean the streets or collect the trash. An oppressive culture.

I am a lifelong Democrat but when I board the aircraft and the pilot comes on the horn and welcomes us from the cockpit, I want to feel that he or she is a Republican. I want him or her to be crisp and authoritative and have military experience. I don't want anyone like me up front. No kidding. Aviators, only.

My Democrats became a cheerless bunch of agonizers in 2017, obsessed about the gentleman who had succeeded our cheerful president, a real estate developer who, as the British writer Nate White points out, "has no class, no charm, no coolness, no credibility, no compassion, no wit, no warmth, no wisdom, no subtlety, no sensitivity, no self-awareness, no humility, no honor and no grace," which is true enough but that's over now, an old newsreel, and now is the problem we must deal with.

Ralph, the country needs you more than ever. Put away yesterday's absurdities and take hold of today with high spirits, forgetting your old nonsense. Today invites us to high hopes—it can be the best day in the year and our time can be a very good time if we will simply do our best with it. And then we have tomorrow to look forward to.

Emerson said, "Live in the sunshine, swim the sea, drink the wild air." And his student Thoreau said, "If one advances confidently in the direction of his dreams, and endeavors to live the life which he has imagined, he will meet with a success unexpected in common hours." This from a man with a face like a pile of fence posts who never had a romance, whose best books sold by the dozens, who died a failure at 44. But the booming drum roll of "If one advances confidently" still rings true today. It's us, it's thoroughly American. I come from stoical people, a stoicism that could be diagnosed as depression, but still, deep in our hearts, we harbor gaudy dreams, if not for ourselves, then for our grandchildren. They will inherit a planet deep into climate change and a culture of cheap leatherette politics—it's a long way from the Dare To Dream era that I grew up in. But I have faith that if the young adopt Emersonian cheerfulness as a strategy, they can make a way through the dark forest. What can't be fixed by legislative action may be solved by the ingenuity of science and engineering. Monster vacuum cleaners that collect plastic molecules and meld them into roadways. One can hope.

Blunders? Tell me about it. I moved from an $80,000 house I loved to a million-dollar house I hated. I wasted a year writing a dreadful opera. I had no patience for rehearsal, believing in spontaneity as I did, and gave many lousy half-hearted performances, which I remember clearly to this day. I married two different women I had never had a long thoughtful conversation with, we simply lurched into marriage on the basis of longing, and then came a long period of pretending to be happy, followed by the chilly dissolution. I walked away from my calling to go live in Copenhagen and act Danish while walking around with a big red A around my neck. I've known episodes of stunning stupidity and at this age I know I'll never be that dumb again. Once I got myself a cabin in the woods of Wisconsin with a separate workroom, 10x15, on stilts, no house or highway in sight, just a big window looking into the trees, where deer sometimes stopped and studied me. After a year I concluded that peace and quiet made me uneasy. And then I met Jenny, a New Yorker, and that was the end of the experiment and the beginning of a long marriage to a graceful humorous woman who also can fix things. She has smaller fingers and can assemble parts into a harmonious whole. I am a writer and the problem of assembly puts me into a subjunctive mood and what I assemble is a non sequitur and somewhere a child is weeping bitterly and wolves are howling outside the cabin.

I was an English major and looked down on the engineering students with the crewcuts, their green plaid shirts with plastic pocket protectors, their slide rules in holsters, and I let my hair grow long because theirs was short and now we live in a digital world these nerds designed: Google, Facebook, and the ATM that shoots money at you like bubbles from a pipe, and this little gizmo the size of half a sandwich that is a camera, encyclopedia, newspaper, calendar, compass, magnifying glass, weather monitor, phone book, search engine for nearby shops and services, and also incidentally a telephone, plus other functions I need my wife to explain to me, the one who reads directions. I used to resent competence and now I'm married to it.

A man craves leadership and my love tells me if there's spinach in my teeth. "Smile," she says, and I do, and there is. I read aloud to her the stuff I've written and if she laughs, I feel noticed, like a peacock I once saw walk across a yard, his great fan of bejeweled feathers open wide, following a peahen whom he had a crush on, and he stretched out his gaudy neck and shook the little doodads on his head and waved the great fan of iridescent blue-green beauty and she looked up and noticed. This happens to me when I read her something I just wrote, like this very paragraph about the peacock, and she laughs out loud at the thought of me as a large bird with a head full of doodads. If I taught Creative Writing, I wouldn't emphasize creativity, I'd teach the importance of marrying the right person.

11

So How's It Going Then?

After getting my pig valve, I was released from St. Mary's and flew back to New York, reading Emerson, where he says that the mark of wisdom is to live in the present and see the world with new eyes, to see the miraculous in the commonplace, and I felt the plane's steep descent and lifted the window shade and saw the dense overcast, no lights visible below even as our wheels were lowered, and down, down, down we came through the soup as the ride got bumpy and then sort of turbulent, dozens of agnostics behind me praying intently to the Eternal Whomever, lights finally appearing a few hundred feet below, a river of headlights on a freeway, the plane shaking as the ground came up to meet us, red lights on the tarmac, and the wheels hit and the nose came down and he reversed the engines and braked hard and brought us around to the terminal at LaGuardia.

Thanks to Emerson, it was rather thrilling, the miracle
of the ordinary. Planes land somewhere every minute. To
see with new eyes the zero visibility and anticipate calmly
the end of my life and hope for an obit that doesn't use
the word "nostalgic," and then the wheels touch down
and we roll to the gate. We won't be on the news tonight,
the governor won't need to issue a statement of sorrow.
Life continues. I hoist my briefcase, thank the captain
standing in the cockpit door ("Cultivate the habit of
gratitude," says Ralph. "Give thanks continuously.")
and I walk up the Jetway and past Starbucks and the
ATMs and the candystand and out the door into the
dark and drizzle and stand in the taxi line and hop in
a cab and into Manhattan we go, down dark streets of
brownstones, a few hardy souls walking their dogs, and
across the Park to the West Side. Gratitude is in order.
And a new day awaits.

An amazing city, sheer mass and density of it, the
grandeur of it, the charm of Victorian streets among the
towers. The vast network of underground rail lines without which the city'd come to a standstill. The municipal
plumbing that brings water and takes away sewage for
the eight million. The interlocking networks of skilled
workers who operate social services, clean the buildings,
enforce the laws, haul away trash, deliver food and neces-
sities. To millions of Americans from here to Hawaii,
the city is Babylon, Doom Town, Batman's Gotham, a

hotbed of crime and corruption, but to the guy in the back seat of the cab, it's a city of the everyday, the corner café, Strand Bookstore, the newsstand, the rumble of the subway. I come home to the lady who opens the door and we stand in our little vestibule, the joyous red Navajo rug hanging on the wall and I put my arms around this slight woman, my chin on her head. We head for the kitchen, she pours a glass of wine, I pour a glass of ginger ale, we go out on the terrace and look out over the rooftops. And so life resumes. A safe landing in every sense of the word.

Now of my three-score years and ten,
Eighty will not come again.
I've passed my expiration date.
I am living, not "the late,"
And since I'm taken with this lady
I'm okay with being eighty
Standing on this New York terrace.
Who needs London, Rome, or Paris?
   I hold her closely to my heart,
   Now working with a porcine part.

It's true. I keep telling myself: I'm 80. I've been around the block. In other civilizations, I would sit cross-legged in my lodge, my beard six feet long, my silvery hair in a bun, and young people would approach me, bowing, bringing gifts, and ask my counsel.

Hey.
Hey. Wear R U?
Talking to an old dude.
OMG. Y?
He wants to put me in his book.
Kewl.
Later.

Young people don't do this so I'm writing the book without their input. Somehow I hope they'll get the message. Cheer up. As Dr. Nash once said about my skinned knee, "It looks worse than it is." Live your life. Follow your heart. It's okay to march but don't forget to dance. Google "R.W. Emerson" sometime, you might take a liking to him.

Coming back to New York after my August stay at St. Mary's, I missed the Minnesota State Fair, our annual cheerfulness exposition to show us Northerners, mournful by nature, who thrive on cold and cloudiness, what giddy pleasure is like. Put us in a cold fog and we bloom. We wave away compliments and are good at suppressing feelings, our own and other people's, but the Fair is our escape from ourselves, mobs of people feasting on deep-fried cheese curds and admiring pigs the size of VWs and riding on something like a giant salad spinner while screaming to high heaven. We wander among giant John Deere tractors and displays of championship quilts and art made by gluing seeds to plywood, and in all the milling around and waiting in line and consumption of animal fats, there is no detectable polarization. Theoretically 33 percent of these people despise another 33 percent while the remainder try to remain indifferent, but you'd never know it walking around the fairgrounds. Some political candidates have booths and stand and talk to their supporters but there's no bitterness, no yelling, no angry signage. The gentleman making milkshakes in the Dairy Building says pleasantly, "So how's your day going then?" though he's probably made five hundred shakes already. His sentence, beginning with "So" and ending with "then," indicates that he's a native Minnesotan, not a Canadian or Floridian. I say, "Never better then." I wish I were there at the Fair. I miss it. I used to do a show at the Grandstand and when you heard four thousand people singing, "My country, 'tis of thee, sweet land of liberty, of thee I sing" with the roller coaster in the background, it made me proud to be one of them.

When I was ten, Dad took me to the Fair and gave me $5 and cut me loose and told me to meet him at 6 p.m.

at the Grandstand ramp and it was a great day. I bought a hot dog and a caramel apple but the day was all about mingling and listening to people, a Brethren boy brought up to avoid unbelievers and here I was surrounded by them. I stood in a crowd watching my mother's hero Cedric Adams deliver his noontime newscast on WCCO from an elevated stage in the Horticulture Building and I stood outside the Harlem Revue, a tent show advertising dancers and a jazz band, and the freak show on the Midway, and admired the barkers' spiels. I considered the double Ferris wheel but didn't fork over the dough. At 6 p.m. I still had two dollars left over. So much of my childhood has vanished in the haze of time, but that day is quite clear and I do believe it was the happiness that made it memorable, the pleasure of anticipating being grown up and walking freely wherever I wished, a lone observer mingling with the humanity, passing through a sea of conversation. That was the appeal of the Fair. People from small towns congregating in a crowd, not to look at exhibits so much as to be in the flock.

12

The Obit Man

I sit down on a stool at the café counter, order a coffee, black, and French toast and a minute later a man sits down on the stool next to me. I say, "Good morning." He looks away. Maybe he's hard of hearing. (But he's in his twenties.) I say, "Looks like this rain is going to continue all day." No response. But when the waitress asks what he'd like, he orders coffee and scrambled eggs. So what is the problem? Is it me? Do I look like an undercover cop? Is he suffering from depression? Does he have something against the French? No, it's that he's young and hip. Black tunic, expensive jeans, his hair long and tied in a bun. Okay. I get it. I'm an old man. I was young once. (Never hip but I had my moments.) My "Good morning" was not a preface to a monologue about how it was way back then. It was only a recognition of our common humanity. If he prefers to be a shrub or a stone wall, that is his right. But inanimate objects are missing out on so much. Life, for one thing. Oh well. Whatever.

My gloomy years started in high school and extended through the ivy-covered pathways of college. The U gave me enough grimness for a lifetime. I stayed in college too long and mainly learned how to write pretentious term papers about texts I'd only glanced at. I also learned to hate *The Waste Land.* There was pretense everywhere you looked. A job on a daily paper would've been a better education. So one fall I went to work at the St. Paul *Pioneer Press* writing obits.

My city editor, Mr. Walt Streightiff, was hard-nosed about obits. Name of Deceased, Survived By, Member Of, Visitation & Services. "Once you start eulogizing people, there'll be no end to it," he said. He wore a starched white shirt with silk armbands, suspenders, and a bow tie that he tied himself, not a clip-on. He was a city editor right out of a previous century. When he barked, you jumped.

But I grieved for the obituarized and wanted to distinguish them. I wrote an obit for a banker—*Every Halloween he dressed up as a hobo*—and a woman *known for her beautiful cinnamon rolls and her collection of salt and pepper shakers*—and a mailman—*Every summer until he was 82, he swam two miles across White Beat Lake and back home*—which Mr. Streightiff did not like but some of them got past him. I wrote about a doctor who could do a loon call so haunting and beautiful that children imitated it so he organized a loon-call contest and offered cash prizes, and at this Mr. Streightiff said, "Enough. No more." So I waited for him to take his lunch break and I put my obit copy into the Inbox on the copy desk, writing his initials "WS" at the top and it went into the paper. The man was strict because it came with the job but there was a way around him.

I also called up hospitals to find out if the victims of car crashes were still living or not, so I could update the highway death toll. One day a photographer brought me his collection of pictures of dead people, a man decapitated by a train, a woman who jumped off the High Bridge, a man who had blown his head off with a shotgun. He had dozens more he wanted to show me. He thought it was wrong that the paper had a policy against pictures of death. "People need to see this," he said, but I wasn't impressed. I asked Mr. Streightiff to take me off the death beat and he said no so I quit. There just isn't much to be said about death. It's like the teacher who asked the little boy, "What does your daddy do?" *My daddy's dead.* "Well, what did he do before he died?" *He sort of clutched at his chest and tried to talk and then he fell over unconscious and we called the ambulance.*

I regret that I never got to write Walt's obit. He was a relic of an era that was fading fast, when editors could bark, but sensitive editors were coming into the trade and the Lifestyle section leaked onto the front page with articles about the importance of family time and opinion columns became affirming and reviewers became boosters and I saw no future in that sort of journalism, so I got into radio and switched from news to comedy. I got the job at KSJR working the 6 a.m. shift. I got it because nobody else wanted to get up that early. Once I got there, I realized that the farmers listening to me while they looked at the udders of Holsteins did not care to hear my thoughts about the decline of American society, they wanted to hear the one about the engineer sentenced to death by guillotine who lay on the platform but they couldn't get the dang blade to drop on his neck and were about to commute his sentence but he looked up and said, "No, hand me the pliers, I see what the problem is." That one. Followed by "Your Feet's Too Big," a Chopin étude, and the Grateful Dead's "Ripple." It was a turning point in life, when I gave up striving to be brilliant and original and turned to the pleasant work of simple entertainment and felt the satisfaction of usefulness, not so different from being an efficient dishwasher at the Evangeline Hotel when I was 18 and the next fall becoming the autocrat of an enormous parking lot at the University and commanding drivers to pull into the one correct space and not consider alternatives.

13

Let Me Say It Once Again

I'm a privileged man. It's true. My parents loved each other. There was no alcohol in the house, everyone spoke softly. I was content being a middle child, feeling sort of invisible. Our parents did not read books about parenting, and when they gathered with other adults, they didn't talk about us, they had their own interests, which were mysterious to us. They were grown-ups and I looked forward to being one too. They didn't instruct us on how to behave though they sometimes corrected us; we learned by imitating them and other grown-ups.

My parents didn't praise their children—it would've struck me as bizarre if they had. A few of my aunts thought I was special but it was a secret between me and them, nothing to flaunt. So when I grew up, my keen sense of inferiority was an engine that kept me going.

I loved singing bass in the Hopeful Gospel Quartet with Robin and Linda and Kate, but when I stand alone on stage and say, "It's been a quiet week in Lake Wobegon" and launch into a story about a bitter winter and the invasion of a porcupine who Mrs. Hedlund believes embodies the ghost of her grandfather, I'm painfully aware of glitches and wrong turns (*How do I get back to the dog with the dead fish in his mouth, why did I get to the guy on the parasail being dragged underwater by the speedboat, I need to bring back the dog before I bring in the hot-air balloon*) but when I sing duets with Heather Masse, I feel transported. I think Emerson missed out on duet-singing. If he'd ever sung harmony with a woman, he would've discovered the true meaning of transcendence.

Mostly, *Prairie Home* was hard work. Comedy does not come easy, not to a Brethren boy. And in the public-radio world, the show was looked upon as something of an embarrassment, a sideshow meant to pull in dough from yahoos. I went to a couple NPR conventions and remember well the smirks on the faces of classical music announcers. I worked for hours writing *Guy Noir* and *Lives of the Cowboys* and *Ruth Harrison, Reference Librarian* and they, who'd spent years putting a needle on a vinyl record of a symphony and pressing *Start* felt vastly superior to me, a mere comedian. I felt sorry for the poor bastards. They sat in a studio, affected an educated tone, and thanks to the word "classical," they were beyond criticism. I worked to a crowd in a theater and got to hang out with them afterward. There were truck drivers, teachers, cops, farmers, dental hygienists, priests, you name it, we had some in the crowd. I could be critical of the show itself but meeting the audience face-to-face set my head on straight: the show was important to them, it made them feel good. Public radio specialized in musical tragedy, academic blowhards, and newscasts with a comfy leftward tilt. Our show was cheerful. They looked forward to it. They even came to see it. Nobody goes to a studio to watch someone put a needle on a vinyl disc.

And now, at 80, I look back and feel rather fortunate. I call old friends on the phone and we commiserate about ocular degeneration, and we recall Benson School, or Sarah Youngblood's Shakespeare class at the U, or a dance at Dania Hall on Cedar Avenue and the Paisleys playing acid rock. A good memory is a great editor. I've forgotten all the committee meetings and the rivalries and jealousies and casual friendships and I recall with stunning clarity, the exact words my mother said that day back in 1951, after she and Dad had fussed at each other about something, a hissy argument, then he left for work, and she stood at the door and said, "Someday that man and I are going to come to a parting of the ways." I ran upstairs and threw myself on my bed and wept and she came up and hugged me and said, "I'm sorry, I didn't mean it. I love him." Which she did. Those five minutes are clear to me but I have very little recollection of the turbulent middle years flying around in the arms of ambition—Jenny tells me about something that happened and I don't remember it and she says, "That's because you were never around."

And then when I was 75 I got kicked off public radio and I became cheerful almost immediately. It was a simple shakedown scheme by a man and woman who'd worked for the show for years—"pay us a million bucks or we'll say bad things about you"—and MPR, without bothering to interview the perps simply cashiered the old man, and it was oddly liberating to be canceled. I walked around St. Paul and people avoided me, which was okay by me. I was no longer that guy on the radio, I was just myself. Around the same time, I gave up driving because my eyesight was poor. Driving was a privilege that used to mean the world to me and now, I discovered, meant almost nothing. A revelation. And unjust humiliation shows you who your true friends are, which is crucial knowledge for anyone but especially for a public figure.

Time is passing swiftly and in recognition of that, I cut back on things. I go for weeks without reading the

news. It's too laborious for a man my age. I write this
as my daughter stands at the kitchen counter, slicing a
banana to put on a bowl of bran flakes for my breakfast.
She is 25 and will survive me by a good stretch and I
want her to remember me as a cheerful man. She often
asks me to make her laugh and I do my best. *Why do
gorillas have large fingers? Because they have large nostrils.*
Knock knock. *Who's there?* Amish. *Amish who?* That's
funny, you don't look like a shoe.

I am a man of privilege, including the privilege of
adversity. I worked early morning shifts for years and so
went to bed early and omitted debauchery. Instead of
smoking dope and writing hallucinatory verse, I slept
and in the morning stood in the snow and commanded
drivers to park where I told them to go. It was good for a
freethinker like me to learn the skills of authoritarianism
and bend others to my will.

I learned the art of invisibility to avoid bullies such
as the Durbin boys. I never got in a fistfight, never
wrote graffiti on a wall, never had a therapist. Suicide
never crossed my mind. My psychic résumé is sort
of thin. But I've been above the Arctic Circle, played
Carnegie Hall, canoed the upper Mississippi, and visited
Mark Twain's house in Hartford, the Grand Ole Opry,
the Little Big Horn, Hemingway's grave, the Giant Slide

at the Minnesota State Fair, and once had dinner with S.J. Perelman and coffee with Lawrence Ferlinghetti. I was baptized by total immersion, head to toe. I read *War and Peace* when I was 16, I dodged the draft, I made the *Times* bestseller list, I learned to make a martini, and I once sang the *Whiffenpoof Song* at a funeral in Washington attended by Bill and Hillary and the ber-obed Justices of the Supreme Court who sat, lips zipped, as everyone else sang "We are little black sheep who have gone astray." I once stood backstage for a show honoring the 100th birthday of Irving Berlin, who wasn't there but Frank Sinatra was, Ray Charles, Tony Bennett, Shirley MacLaine, Willie Nelson, Bob Hope, Leonard Bernstein, Rosemary Clooney, famous people jammed in together and so stunned by the company they were in, they acted normal. I don't know anyone who has a similar résumé. Maybe draft-dodging and Carnegie Hall but not total immersion and lunch with Perelman and singing to the Supreme Court, all three.

It was the Durbins' softball team I played against when I dropped the pop fly. I was the first baseman. Years later, an ophthalmologist told me I have a case of "Duane syndrome," which is double vision while look-ing up, and I flashed back to that pop-up bouncing off my skull in fourth grade, which led to recess in the library and books and the ambition to be a writer and this cheery life I lead today.

discovered *The New Yorker* in eighth grade and decided A.J. Liebling was the real deal and I read everything he'd written about New York and Paris and the war, then discovered John Updike and Charles Portis. My classmates were in choir, band, debate, theater, sports; I read Edith Oliver, Andy Logan, Lillian Ross. I needed a job to pay for college so I got into radio thanks to my imitation of the buttery baritone of Robert Trout of CBS and Chet Huntley of NBC. I sat in a small studio with green acoustic tile on the walls and looked up through a slanted glass window to the engineer in the control room and the *ON AIR* light flashed and though I wore jeans and a sweatshirt I sounded like a three-piece herringbone suit from Hart, Schaffner & Marx. It was an easy job and it came with a handsome office looking out on stately buildings with columns and a grassy quad but it was stupefying work in a listless environment. The U gave me a keen aversion to bureaucracy, the endless powwow, the power of the chief and his shamans, the claustrophobic warrens of academe, the trawling at parties, the schmoozing and butt-kissing. So I upped and quit. I had no money and I quit an easy job that paid well. It was one of the great decisions of my life, that and the lunch with the young violinist years later, but that's a different story.

I was 27, I had wasted enough time. I wanted to be a writer but nobody wanted to publish what I wrote so

I felt unappreciated but people don't appreciate writing about being unappreciated so I decided to go back to radio because it simply is what it is. The microphone comes on and you say something into it. And I have a gloomy face so I never could've gotten a job in sales and I wasn't smart enough to be a teacher so, I headed for KSJR at St. John's University.

I mailed a batch of stories off to a famous magazine at 25 West 43rd Street in New York and went up to St. John's where the manager, Bill Kling, was my age, but dressed like a manager in dark blue suit and white shirt, narrow tie, and he looked at me in a flowery shirt and fringed vest, leather boots and bell-bottoms, chain-smoking, bearded, unkempt and yet pretentious, but I was the only applicant, so I got the job.

It was the Continental Divide of my life, where I escaped the meritocracy and jumped the tracks and went skittering into radio with the freedom to be light-hearted—which was unknown territory in public radio at the time—and to play Jelly Roll Morton and the Jubilee Quartet and *catch a wave and you're sitting on top of the world* amid the fugues and études, plus Jew's-harp blues and Sousa played on a kazoo and roll out the barrel, a bit of a Brandenburg, and Bob Wills. My theme song was "Bugle Call Rag"—*You're bound to fall for the bugle call; you're gonna brag 'bout the Bugle Call Rag.* I played requests, wished a woman named Rhonda a happy birthday and played "Help Me, Rhonda," it was a loose and friendly show sponsored by Powdermilk Biscuits and Ralph's Pretty Good Grocery ("If we don't have it, you can get along without it"), and then one day came the astonishing letter from Roger Angell at *The New Yorker* buying a story of mine and that changed everything. Two big golden doors swung open and I walked through. End of Act One, cue the clown band, the spangly lady, and the acrobats for Act Two.

This is the luxury of old age, you look back fifty years and see how your life was shaped by a dropped ball and a trip to New York. And by Dr. Frank Mork refusing to allow me to play football—"You have a clicky heart," he said, a piece of wild good luck. I didn't really want to play, I only wanted to be a normal Anoka boy, but I would've been a timid player and gotten good and concussed and today I wouldn't be able to write this sentence, but instead I got hired by Warren Feist at the Anoka *Herald* to write sports for $2 a game and I smelled the hot lead of the Linotype and the ink of the rotary press and the whiskey on the pressman's breath and saw my name in print—Gary E. Keillor—and life took a different direction. Thank God for failure. My friends of Viking heritage breathe the September air and feel a powerful urge to get in a longboat and go burn a village and capture all the women and I have no Viking blood in me, I've been tested for it. I come from humble Yorkshire stock, with some Welsh and Huguenot on the Powell side, and my mother's ancestors from the Scottish slums.

At age 96, Mother told me, "There's so much I'd still like to know but there's nobody left to ask." A great line. All her twelve siblings who had lived in the big house on Longfellow Avenue were gone. She was an old lady with snow-white hair brushed back, almost blind, her skin papery, reaching out to put her wrinkled hand on my hand. On her bedside table was a photograph of four young ladies in their summer dresses, straddling their bicycles, grinning, in 1936. She was the one on the left. There's much more I'd like to know too, but I'm grateful for the pig valve in my heart and YouTube where Don and Phil Everly sing "Stories We Could Tell," and Sam Hudson at the wheel driving us to another theater somewhere to do another show, and my "Minnesota" coffee mug with the loon on a lake, and the coffee in it, also the excellent Micron 02 pen in my hand and the yellow legal pad, and don't forget the woman who put a hand on my shoulder and said she adores me, which makes me feel like the vintage wine I read about that has "a light velvety body with persistent effervescence, robust but subtle, and a crisp, clean palate enhanced by earthy complexity." It's not easy being robust but subtle, but she brings out the effervescence in me and also the complexity (I always was earthy).

14

It's About Time

Whenever I step out on the street, I recognize that I am Mr. Yesterday, a leftover from the fermented generation that sang "We Shall Overcome" and did not, a person of interest only to other geriatrics. Obscurity falls upon us like a gentle snowfall. An agent tried to sell the idea of a Lake Wobegon series to cable TV and found that nobody in the industry had ever heard of it. Fans of *Prairie Home* asked me to come do a benefit for their local school and I said yes and a very nice person from the school called and asked, "What is it exactly that you do?" The world moves on, as it should.

Young people pass at a brisk pace while texting 60 w.p.m. on tiny cellphone touchpads as they're tuned in to Egyptian rappers on their headphones chanting hieroglyphic lyrics and my generation sang "All we are saying is, Give peace a chance," words that make no sense, and now we're irrelevant. Our grandchildren who will have to deal with our mess will look back at the early 21st century as the Era of Stupidification. Meanwhile, I feel relieved to be irrelevant. Young people are thinking about the future of the planet, and I am thinking about buying blueberries to put on my bran flakes. Each life is a work of art and theirs is an enormous mural and mine is an etching. I live in a bubble. I never shot a man in Reno just to watch him die, as Johnny Cash did, or shot the sheriff, like Bob Marley. I used to shoot baskets and now I shoot the breeze. I look at newspaper headlines and I think, "Not My Problem." I'm tired of being appalled. Like the old gospel song says, "This world is not my home, I'm only passing through," and it feels good to be a tourist. I skip the lecture about global warming and the stand-up comedy, which is about bad boyfriends, and I go to the circus and see the spangly woman do a one-handed handstand on a man's upraised forehead and minutes later a woman on the flying trapeze hurls herself into a triple forward flying somersault and into the hands of the catcher, no safety net below. My heart stops and then it starts again.

I read about Sir Walter Raleigh, a classic overachiever, handsome poet, stylish dresser, eager soldier, a favorite at Elizabeth's court, who sailed up the Orinoco in search of El Dorado and failed and sailed back to London to be thrown in prison and have his head chopped off, a warning to the rest of us: there is such a thing as Much Too Much Good. When everything is coming up roses, beware: you can't live on roses, they're inedible. It was a long fall for a great man, from queen's favorite to a city in North Carolina. But he'd said as much in his lines:

"Even such is time, which takes in trust
Our youth, our joys, and all we have,
And pays us but with age and dust."

Dark lines indeed, and I'd only point out that he was imprisoned in comfortable quarters in the Tower of London, not a dungeon cell but a room with a view, and his wife lived with him and conceived a child, so Walter could've revised his poem to read: ... *And pays us but with age and dust/though even so we find a few/ flagons of wine and waves of lust/overcome us two and cheerfully we screw.*

I am old enough to have seen the ancient Albert Woolson, the last living veteran of the Civil War, in a convertible in a parade in Minneapolis. I saw New York City in 1953 and ate at an Automat and saw a Broadway show for a ticket that cost five bucks. I babysat at the Andersons' so I could watch the *Jackie Gleason Show* on their TV, the screen the size of a cereal bowl, he glaring at Audrey Meadows and saying, *One of these days, Alice—pow! Right in the kisser!* which was funny then and is not anymore. I watched the coronation of Queen Elizabeth II on a TV brought to Benson School for the occasion and I loved the horses pulling her carriage, they reminded me of Uncle Jim's. I got to visit the farm and stand on a hayrack with him and hold the reins and when he jumped down to open the gate, I cried, "Giddup!" and they giddupped. I saw my beloved grandma wring a goose's neck with two brisk twists and chop its head off—she didn't tell me to turn my head, she simply did what she needed to do. I walked past the Alvin burlesque theater downtown and stared at posters of large ladies in gaudy foundation garments. I sang "Softly and Tenderly Jesus Is Calling" on a downtown street corner as the preacher Leslie Grant used a loudspeaker on the roof of his car to tell passersby to give their lives to the Lord, and nobody stopped to accept Jesus, they walked past quickly as if we were lunatics and they were afraid we'd clutch them and not let go. I remember the 15¢ White Castle hamburger. I remember seeing hitchhikers on the highway and Dad slowing down and if the guy looked decent, we gave him a lift.

I miss the old days. I miss the light bulb jokes. Somebody would tell one—*How many psychiatrists does it take to change a light bulb? (One but the light bulb has to really want to change.)*—and then other people would contribute and you'd get a whole string of them—*Irishmen.*

(One to hold the bulb, nine to drink until the room spins.)
Jewish mothers. (None. I'll just sit in the dark and suffer.)
Episcopalians. (None, we have candles.) Amish. (What
light bulb?) Germans. (Nein.) Comedians. (It's not funny!)
Comedy in chain reaction.

I miss humor columns in newspapers, like Dave
Barry's. Dave pointed out the fact that men will never
ask for directions, which is why it takes several million
sperm to find one female egg even though, compared
to them, it is the size of Wisconsin. I laughed so hard
at that, I almost coughed up a hairball. He once made
fun of Grand Forks, North Dakota, whereupon the city
fathers invited Dave to Grand Forks, and Dave, classy
guy that he was, flew to Grand Forks for the dedication
of a municipal sewage pump station named after him.
The plaque reads "Dave Barry Lift Station No. 16."

These features are all gone, along with the old yellow
trolleys in Minneapolis with the glass coinbox and the
conductor dinging the bell and the long arm riding on
the overhead wires that gave off sparks. They ran along
Bloomington Avenue in front of our house and I sat on
the steps and imagined becoming a motorman, a noble
aspiration. I went to school before they introduced
tracking, when the ambitious kids were in the same class
with the goof-offs, we were all squashed together, we
weren't encouraged to imagine we were superior to others. In God's eyes, we are all sparrows. We all stood up

first thing and pledged allegiance to the same flag, there wasn't a separate one for math whizzes.

As the great Van Morrison wrote:
The beauty of the days gone by
It brings a longing to my soul
To contemplate my own true self
And keep me young as I grow old.

"I was lucky to live when I did," I often think to myself. With no social media, everything was up close and personal. There was less paranoia, terrorism being so rare. Prosperous times and I got to witness the satisfaction of my elders who, having endured the Depression and survived the war, found romance and employment and could afford to buy a bungalow with a garage and screened porch and a backyard to grill hot dogs in and the kids play catch. We picked vegetables from our garden and cooked them in a pressure cooker and packed them in Ball jars with Kerr lids, quart jars of corn and beans and tomatoes. I was on hand when doo-wop, R&B, rock 'n' roll came rolling in to destroy the country or save it, take your pick. I heard the news on the radio the morning Buddy Holly died in the plane crash. I saw the Rolling Stones play at a hockey rink on their first American tour and, God bless them, they're still playing "Brown Sugar" and "Tumbling Dice" better than any bar band around, Mick Jagger strutting and flapping around, 80 going on 17. I remember Sal (The Barber) Maglie, Whitey Skoog, Rocky Marciano, Sugar Ray Robinson, and Slammin' Sammy Snead. I saw Rod Carew steal home. Twice. I was around for the corner grocer, the stationery shop, the independent druggist, the five & dime, before Amazon took over the world. I wrote letters in a nice cursive hand to my grandma and she was happy and complimented me on my penmanship. A good hand was a sign of good manners. Now grandmas are happy if you're not nonbinary and your face is clear of tattoos.

Back then we heard the buzzin' of the bees in the cigarette trees near the lemonade springs where the bluebird sings, it was way back before seat belts when I stood on the front seat, my hand on Daddy's shoulder as he drove 75 mph across North Dakota and even today I don't buckle up until the buzzer goes off. I know how to drive a car with a standard stick transmission. I am one of the few authors still respirating who typed out stories on an Underwood typewriter and sent them to magazines in an envelope, with a self-addressed envelope enclosed, keeping a carbon copy for personal reference. I was edited by the late William Shawn of *The New Yorker* and he wrote precise suggestions signed "WS" in the margins of the galley proofs and he was almost always right. I know the Minnesota state song and am happy to sing it. I put myself through college working part-time and graduated with no debt, and since I owed my parents nothing, I could aspire to be a writer, which of course dismayed them, thinking of what happened to Fitzgerald and Hemingway.

Friends of mine are dismayed by octogenarianism and don't want to hear about it but for me it's new and fascinating, as if I'd been shipped to Nantes. I have no idea where to start becoming French but now I'm here so I'll have to figure it out. Get the lowdown. *Obtenez la vérité.* The *Marseillaise* is quite a number (do you salute with your left hand or right?). I'll have to learn *Était-ce moi ou était-ce toi?* (Was that me or was it you?) *Je vais bien, je ne peux pas me plaindre.* (I'm okay, can't complain.) *Quoi de neuf, bouton d'or?* (What's up, buttercup?) *Avoir une emprise.* (Get a grip.)

When I was young, I didn't consider old age an attractive option because it meant crankiness and complaints about "what are these kids doing on my lawn?" but old age came along anyway so now I try to accept change. The old warehouse/printing district of Minneapolis where ink-stained men trundled giant rolls of paper into the big presses and the ground shook as the presses turned and truckloads of seed catalogs and hunting magazines pulled out onto Washington Avenue now is the condo/espresso/IT district where highly caffeinated people stare at screens and conceptualize.

I know few people who work with their hands, just their fingers. Me too. I got a computer and shortly thereafter my typewriter went into the closet and the door was closed. The computer made a squiggly blue line under "Levetiracetem" until I spelled it correctly: Levitiracetam. The typewriter didn't care one way or the other. Google "Thou preparest a table before me in the presence of mine enemies" and it will give you the whole psalm and if you poke around you'll find that David the psalmist, having seen the naked Bathsheba, seduced her and then sent her husband into battle to die—in other words, the guy who wrote "The Lord is my shepherd, I shall not want" could be a real jerk and his Shepherd must've wanted to throw him off a cliff but did not. You can also look up the Gadsden Purchase or the Smoot-Hawley Act or the great Nichols & May sketch in which he kisses her passionately and while locked in the kiss she opens the corner of her mouth and exhales cigarette smoke. Instant results, no waiting. With search engines at our fingertips, it's a wonder we aren't smarter than we are.

My dad got his exercise by gardening and doing carpentry and working on his car and my mom did squats and stretches, vacuuming and scrubbing and checking on pies in the oven. Now people hire personal trainers to coax them to do stuff that once was necessary to maintain civilized life. Maybe our grandkids will own butt-bots to wipe themselves and also brush their teeth. I take no position for or against this but I am glad to be living now and not somewhere in the future tense when innovations will likely appear that would horrify me if I were alive, which I won't be so what's the problem?

And YouTube: you can toss your 45s, all the great hits of my teen years are there, waiting to be savored. And Bruce Springsteen singing "Purple Rain." And there's the lady in the dashboard directing my wife through twisting 18th-century streets in New England as my daughter in the back seat FaceTimes her roommate Saamiya visiting relatives in India. My girl is thrilled by her busy social life and the old man is amazed to hear India in the car—long-distance but we don't even use the term anymore—and in our capitalist society, why does this not cost $35.75 a minute? A miracle. And advances in medicine extended my life beyond that of my poor uncles. I was short of breath and ceme-tery-bound, there were bouquets of lilies with my name on them, the minister was looking forward to a good crowd, but the surgical team opened me up and sewed the mitral valve and I was good to go. My demise was put off for a time. I'm truly grateful. I've enjoyed the extension, the writing, the sleeping, the thousands of Scrabble games with Jenny especially the six or seven that I won.

everal of us old grumblers like to meet for lunch at a café in an old part of town where young people go, and one sees signs of incipient romance, couples venturing into conversation, leaning toward each other, putting a hand on the other's arm. We watch, we remember.

Sometimes I get to hang out with young people, which they let me do because I pick up the check. I like them, they're warped forward, all about today and tomorrow and the Sixties are way back next door to the Civil War. I enjoy listening to them talk. "Sketchy"—I like that word. *That's sketchy.* Girls say to another girl: *Hey, lady.* And they say to a guy: *Just man up.* "Where you at?" *I'm all stressed. Well, get over it. Blah blah blah.* Keep things light. Dating is too serious, so they *hang out.* They say, *Too much information. T.M.I. Too much drama.* They love the word *actually.* Actually they do but also ironically. *Really.* You try to b.s. them, they say, *Shut up. (No way.) Whatever. Take a chill pill. Get a life.* I love that. We didn't say *Get a life* back in my day, it just wasn't available. I don't care for *OMG* or *awesome* (it's so over) but *get a life*—that is *perfect. Sweet.* They're sweet kids. They're good to go. *Totally.* My generation never said "totally"; we didn't dare think in terms of entirety, we enjoyed the good parts of the movie—it was okay—but now you can be totally into it, all over it, it's awesome. (We knew the word "awesome" but never said it.) But now I'm 80, I've got a life, more life than anyone else at this table, I'm into it, totally. Scarcity makes the days awesome. So deal with it. And the waitress slips me the check and I totally pay it. Gladly. Really.

Women stride past me on the street, saying, "On your left," in a hurry to get to a meeting somewhere and fight the good fight for the true and beautiful and I have no appointments, no Mr. Big Pants is waiting to tell me my proposal has been declined. I'm free as a kid. I could hop on the A train and ride out to Far Rockaway and watch the Atlantic roll in on the shore and observe planes descending toward JFK and I wouldn't even need to invent an excuse.

Instead, I board the downtown C train and a young woman boards and stands in front of me, her black tights and dancerly legs, her tank top, and I look at her face for the three seconds permissible and she is actually quite standout beautiful. She studies me for any indications of perversity and then seats herself next to me, four inches apart. I wish she'd say, "I loved your radio show," but no such luck. I'd like to strike up a conversation, one friendly guy talking to his neighbor, and I think about it ("How's your day going so far?") and no reasonable neighborly line comes to mind. ("Are you a dancer? You look so much like Shirley MacLaine." And she'd say, "Who?") "Get over yourself," I think and I do. A woman who looks like her gets more than enough noise from men so why be one more irritation? She's probably stuck in a stupid job manning (womaning) the Information desk in a lobby in Midtown, waiting to get called for an audition. She's an actor and she came from Utah four months ago and lives in a fifth-floor walk-up with three roommates, one with a drug problem and another with a sick cat and a bad boyfriend, and she's thinking of ditching them and finding a new place and she knows a boring guy who is interested in a romantic relationship, and what do I possibly have to contribute to all this? Nothing. I'd like to offer encouragement but I'm afraid it would strike her as weird and that would be dreadful. And she can hear me thinking and she gets off at 50th and I at 42nd, two lives meet briefly and part without a word spoken.

I'm grateful for my pig valve that extends my long life and for RhymeZone, moving sidewalks, 24-hour dry cleaning, Grubhub, color inversion of text files, and seat warmers, which have changed life in the North: a cold morning but in five minutes your butt is warm and it's like falling in love. Some other new developments I ignore. Back in my day, only carnival workers and former felons wore tattoos and now half the young women I see do. *Okay then.* In my day, you said, "Thank you" and they said, "You're welcome." Now they say, "No problem." I grew up in a household where profanity never raised its blunt head and now very nice children talk like angry truckers. I ignore it. People come to visit and every few minutes they check their phone for messages. I make no comment. Some of my heroes are dead but I keep finding new ones, like my friend Heather who, a few years ago, came to New York to sing at the Blue Note downtown, bringing her one-year-old daughter who was taking steps, holding on to a chair, launching out across the floor to her mama, her comforter, dairy bar, wiper, valet, and when she arrived at her mother's pant leg, the child looked up at me to make sure I noticed. The mother did the gig, arose cheerfully to catch an early flight home, packed up a stroller, folding crib, suitcase, backpack, headed out the door with an independent-minded toddler, no problem. It was a vision of cheerful competence such as keeps the trains running and the hospitals open and the schools sending out cheerful replacements into the world.

15

Leaving Home

I love Minnesota. I am Minnecentric and always will
be. Most people know little about it except that it gets
cold in the winter and so wherever you go, you begin
with a clean slate. New Yorkers don't even know where
approximately it is, somewhere out near Chicago. We
Minnesotans have a reputation for being nice, thanks to
Mr. Walter Mondale, but he had his salty side too. He
once told a friend of mine who asked if he should go to
work in a big law firm: "You'll spend four years kissing
ass and they won't even turn around and say, Thank you."
Kissing ass is not popular here. Mutual respect is.

The state is on America's front line of defense against
Canada, we're the home of Hazelden and the recovery
industry, offering recovery groups for people in grief at
pet loss, short people, Scandophrenics, vegephobes, the
compulsively colorless, people suffering from northpolar

disorder and traumatic taciturnity, hypercalmness, disagreement anxiety, disaster anticipation—you name it and there's a program for you where you will hear a talk and then break up into discussion groups, but there is no group for old men at the high end of the contentment spectrum. We are on our own.

I pulled out of Minnesota when I was 80 because I needed a fresh start in a place where I don't belong. For forty years I lived in St. Paul on a bluff over the Mississippi valley, looking down at the railroad tracks where my dad rode the North Coast Limited twice a week, in the mail car, a .38 pistol on his hip, sorting mail into sacks to be hurled out the door in cities and towns as the train whistled through. My mother, Grace, in her late teens, lived a few blocks away and earned pocket money going door to door selling peanut butter cookies in brown lunch bags. The two of them are buried in a little cemetery above a creek that flows into the Rum River, which flows into the Mississippi near where I was born. Someday I'll be buried there too, unless I fall off a fishing boat off the coast of Connecticut and am eaten by sharks.

Some of us don't get far in this world. I graduated from the University of Minnesota on the riverbank in Minneapolis, where now I go to hockey games and the pep band plays "Minnesota, hats off to thee, to thy colors true we shall ever be," same as back in 1964, and I stand

and sing it, which I didn't back then because I was a poet
and loyal only to myself. In Manhattan I am anonymous,
just as I was when I was an undergrad, which makes me
feel young and ambitious. I fall asleep in Manhattan
and my old relatives are in my dreams. I walk through
a garden of tomato plants and strawberries and Eleanor
and Josephine and Bessie approach and we walk arm in
arm. All is forgiven. We stand around a piano, standing
close, arms around each other, Mother playing, we sing
"Standing on the Promises." I hope to have a dream in
which my father puts an arm around me but he has not
yet found a way to do that. As for New York, it is friendly
but it isn't family. I can have engaging conversations with
people I know here but they don't find their way into my
dreams. I suppose they're busy.

I liked big houses, had three of them in St. Paul, one
after another, and hosted musicians there and threw
some good parties, forty or fifty people, sometimes a
band playing, Butch or Rich at the piano, some people
danced, and some hung out on the terrace. The hosts
welcomed people at the door, kept an eye out for orphans
and chatted them up, tried to stifle politics. This was
a liberal crowd prone to indignation and anxiety, the
heebie-jeebies, the fantods a communicable virus, and
your job is to keep an ear out for it and try to quash it

and instill silliness, which Minnesotans resist. We are given to earnestness and if someone at the party gets onto the topic of the lack of music education in the primary grades, it will gather a crowd so the host needs to tell jokes, put a doily on his head, squeeze the whoopee cushion in his back pocket, sing "On the Road to Mandalay," anything to keep people lighthearted. It was like hosting the show but harder.

Adopting cheerfulness as a strategy does not mean closing your eyes to evil; it means resisting our drift toward compulsive dread and despond. My mother dreaded seeing me poke a fork into the toaster to fish out a tiny piece of toast, she gasped, she imagined sparks flying and the sizzle of her middle child, like a murderer in the electric chair. So I did it (carefully) when she wasn't looking. I'm disturbed by swaggering men who holler obscenities and gun their engines when the light turns green—I think, "Well, they were slow readers in fourth grade and other kids made fun of them and now in their late forties they're trying to heal the wound." A fiftyish dude in a "White All Right!" T-shirt guns his Harley and heads into the freeway tunnel where he sounds like an Apollo rocket taking off and I think, "Well, that's the problem with tracking in public schools, separating kids into Advanced, Mediocre, and

Food Service Workers. This guy went without history, literature, science, math, and this is what comes of it." A resentful underclass of rejects. Like the mob that invaded the Capitol on January 6, 2021.

My fellow Democrats try to ignore evil; they're busy trying to eliminate reference to gypsy moths lest Romany people feel marginalized and to achieve numerical diversity in the arts and replace cops with social workers, and so forth, but there are angry characters out to create civil dysfunction and make us wary of walking to church on Sunday. They favor the open carrying of arms in public places, which, if it becomes customary, will cast a dark shadow over city life, and some of us Episcopalians will need to consider becoming Epistolarian and carrying a Colt to 10 a.m. Communion. *Shoot if you must, you SOB, but not during prayer or hymnody or when the Holy Word is read, or you'll go down in a hail of lead. Go shoot some horned or furry mammalians, but don't mess with Episcopalians. Even as I sing God's praises, you'll go down as my six-gun blazes. I'm a Christian but I carry heat: next stop for you is the Judgment Seat.*

Jesus wept for the leper, the sick and helpless, the demented, and we grieve for the undocumented migrants whom we need to do the scut work of the slaughterhouse but nonetheless persecute, and the inner-city kids in lousy schools, the mentally ill. We grieve for the schools made into fortresses, anti-vehicle barriers outside public buildings. When I first saw the U.S. Capitol one night in 1962, the doors were open and two cops sat on folding chairs inside and you could walk in and admire the great dome and murals and statuary, as if it all belonged to you. No surveillance, no metal detectors, no uniformed men with assault weapons.

I live on the Upper West Side of Manhattan, which is more like 1962 America, no big police presence, the doormen in the big apartment buildings keep an eye on things but there's no sense of danger lurking in dark alleys due to the fact that there are no alleys to lurk in, you'd need to lurk out in the open. It's a neighborhood of social workers, teachers, union organizers, shrinks, musicians, freelance activists, and the less successful lawyers, who read the *Times* faithfully and grieve for the sorrows of the world and then console themselves with a croissant and a double latte. I stand on our terrace and look at the sun setting over the Hudson and think about the explosion that created the universe 13.7 billion years ago, a universe expanding still, our Milky Way soon to collide with Andromeda, our sun to expire in a mere 5 billion years, and this tells me the cosmos is not serene and our "civilization" is a microscopic footnote. God gives us a few moments here and we should take delight in them and so I do.

I feel the rumble of the trains running under Central Park West: a great innovation of the early 20th century that lets you board a train and be in Midtown in seven minutes. The suburbs of Connecticut and New Jersey came later in the automobile age, and rush hour is a horror, so commuters email and text behind the wheel, shave, do makeup, driving 3 mph, steering with their knees, Zooming with colleagues. Many doctors got their degrees taking online courses while commuting, which means you might go in for a tonsillectomy and come out missing your left lung.

Living in Manhattan isolates us from these harsh realities, besides which I am retired and so every day is Saturday, but I hear stories, I know that the world can come crashing down any day. Not for me, not quite yet, but for other people. People call and tell me these things, all the more so when they find out I'm writing a book about cheerfulness. Some days I feel like I'm the Wailing Wall for Prots, I hear about knee replacements, a lay-off, a despicable minister, an Anglican who married into a family of right-wing evangelicals, a QAnon niece, a classmate sliding into the darkness of dementia, a friend planning a memorial service for his mom's dog. Trouble with a capital T and that rhymes with P and that stands for Protestant. Stories about folks who've been on the job for ten, fifteen years, feeling part of the office family, and then new management comes in and the blade falls.

You worked your way up in the Skin Division of Amalgamated Potato and one day a white envelope appears on your desk and you are now roadkill, a dark smear on the corporate highway. You worked day and night, kissed every ass that was offered, and then the hedge fund that owned AP sold it to fudge fund and they switched from spuds to spaghetti and decimated the workforce to turn humongous profits so the company could be sold to a slush fund and make them dizzy rich, and you, Mr. Potato Head, get a handshake and an offer of a job with the new company if you attend a six-week transformation class at a concrete-origami seminar center with big skylights and indoor trees to learn how a holistic value structure facilitates dynamically through all functions of the organization from the bottom up but then you remember what Emerson said, "When you are shown the door, take it as a window of opportunity," and you head for Alaska and open up a fishing camp. This happened to a guy I know.

People in Alaska do real things all day, and at night they tell stories about them. That's why Alaska is there: to give you an alternative to the monkey island of corporate life. Beyond the grid, the level of b.s., c.s., and h.s. drops sharply as the reality of mountains appears. Dense fogs descend on most organizations and people with porcelain hairnets tell you what to do in a language they themselves have invented and that is the time to get out of town. A classic American solution: put dead history behind you and you'll open up vistas shining and new. It's a big country. Goodbye, Minneapolis, hello, Manhattan.

I know a little about dread. I grew up reading about nuclear devastation, a blazing flash in the sky that would reduce us kids to scorch marks on the sidewalk. My dad fell off a barn roof and fractured his skull and I knew from the sound of Mother's voice that he might die. (He did not. Not then.) A dear cousin was blinded by the sunrise and pulled out on the highway and was killed instantly by a speeding semi. A gifted musician was hit by a stroke, which left him half paralyzed, unable to play, his calling vanished into thin air. I saw my friend Bill Hinkley dying at the VA hospital, miserable from the drugs he was getting, his legs not working right. He asked if I knew "Abide With Me" and so I sang it and he sang with me as I helped him to the toilet, arms around him, sang about the deepening shadows as life's little day ebbs away and other helpers fail and earth's joys grow dim, Lord, Help of the Helpless, abide with me. His misery was profound. There was nothing to do for him except be there. I saw my friend Chet Atkins after he had been mauled by a stroke and a brain tumor and I knew he didn't want me to see him like that, in a wheelchair, wrapped in an overcoat, a guitar on his lap though he couldn't do anything with it. I talked to him about Uncle Dave Macon the Dixie Dewdrop, Maybelle Carter, Red Foley, Hank Williams, people he knew when he was on the way up, and there he sat, a mournful shadow of himself. Then I remembered our tour out west with his band, our chartered jet hit rough air over Colorado, and his guitarist Paul Yandell said, "I can see the headline: Chet Atkins and Garrison Keillor and Four Others Die in Plane Crash. And I'll be one of the others." Chet laughed at that, sort of.

It wasn't depressing to visit the dying, it was a mission: nobody should die alone, we need to see our people to the end of the block. No need for pity, small talk does just fine; tell them about your week, where you went, who you saw, what they said. No bad news. Reminisce, talk about food, tell a joke.

A stroke didn't decimate me: a doctor put me on a blood thinner and Levetiracetam and here I am, writing in a steady hand with a pen on a yellow legal pad, which gives me a basis for gratitude, which is a wellspring of cheerfulness.

Friends ask me, "How are you?" and I say, "Never better." I only have a certain number of friends, some have died or moved to Arizona, two are in Memory Units and don't know me from Genghis Khan or Grace Kelly, so I am counting on these remaining pals to converse with, such as two old guys I knew when I was a kid—our conversations would be meaningful to only about four other people on the planet and when they're gone, I'll have nobody to talk to who remembers the West River Road circa 1951 or Stan Nelson's gym class or could appreciate the thrill of riding in Will Peterson's VW with the Danish exchange student sitting on my lap. My middle decades were turgid, a forest of obligations, but Anoka High is still clear in our minds, the hallways, the lockers, who hung out with whom. Friendship is a secret shared language and friends are irreplaceable, Arvonne, Don, Corinne, Sydney, Bill, Irv, Chet, Paul, Roland, George, Arnie, Bob, Howard, Helen, Jean, Philip, Bruce, all departed. I can hear their voices, I remember them in their cheerful moments, at the wheel of a car, turning to tell me something important and interesting.

Twenty years ago I stood out on West End Avenue at 2:30 a.m. with George Plimpton, hailing a cab, and he said, "Friendship is what it's all about. It's what it's always been about." He'd been drinking Scotch, I was sober, and we were only distant acquaintances, but I was a fan of his books and it had been a wonderful party and it was a fall night and the city felt golden.

He was Exeter, Harvard, his dad was a diplomat, his ancestors came over on the Mayflower, he had an odd accent like his tongue was bandaged; I was Anoka High and U of M, my dad was a railway mail clerk, my people came out of the slums of Glasgow and the woods of Canada, I talk flat Midwestern. He had beautiful manners that put people at ease and at 2:30 a.m., we felt a bond. He had known Hemingway and Ezra Pound and Frost and liked to talk about them and their revels with lady friends. He was a gent whose social circle intersected with the Bushes' but he had gone off to Paris at the age of 26, lived in a toolshed with an army cot, went to the Hôtel Plaza Athénée to steal stationery and write to his parents that he was doing well. He met Jacqueline Bouvier, they drank *vin ordinaire,* he helped found the *Paris Review,* his true love. I'm a Minnesotan with a snooty attitude toward Harvard guys but George had a generous soul and I got over it.

He had a gift for friendship. Writers you admire seem so formidable on first meeting but Maxine Kumin sat and talked about her farm and her horses and W.S. Merwin showed me his palm tree forest on Maui and Jim Harrison talked about his cabin in the Upper Peninsula. Gay Talese said he loved to write on the white cardboard dry cleaners put in folded shirts. S.J. Perelman kvetched about editors. Nora Ephron ran into me on upper Broadway and pointed out the building where Isaac Singer had lived. I met Norman Mailer after his celebrity had faded and he was a very pleasant normal guy. And the first time I met David Sedaris it was like we'd known each other for years. I don't have the gift, having been brought up evangelical, but I've been grateful for people who do, like Ada Louise Huxtable, the architecture critic at the *Times,* who once found me at a dinner, sitting off in a corner, not knowing how to mingle with strangers, and she sat down and rescued me.

I loved her writing, her passion, how she described Lincoln Center as "extravagantly commonplace" and the Kennedy Center in Washington as "a cross between a concrete candy box and a marble sarcophagus in which the art of architecture lies buried." She was an attractive 90-year-old woman, a New Yorker born and bred, and she knew I was from the Midwest and she launched into talking about prairie architecture and Frank Lloyd Wright and the ranch house, which she loved as iconically American and had bought one in Marblehead, Massachusetts, as a summer house and put in a swimming pool, and then was reminded of a story about a Massachusetts politician named Endicott Peabody about whom an opponent said, "He was the only man to have four towns in Massachusetts named for him: Peabody, Athol, Hyannis, and Marblehead." The woman who described one building (I forget which) as "a colossal collection of minimums" saw a stranded stranger and stopped to cheer him up.

This is what makes New York worth the crowds and the clatter, the possibility of suddenly meeting someone fascinating. I once met the editor Eleanor Gould, the legendary grammarian, who was nearly blind and who recognized my voice and announced she was a fan of my show and loved an Irving Berlin song I'd sung recently and so I stood in the hallway and sang it to her, *What'll I do when you are far away and I am blue, what'll I do?* And she complimented me on my good diction.

Across the hall from our apartment was our friend Ira who grew up Jewish in an Italian neighborhood in Brooklyn, learned to mind his manners, did well in school, went to Brooklyn College for $15 a semester, got into law school on a scholarship. Worked in a law firm, hated it, thought about going to grad school to study philosophy, drove cab for a while. "The hardest job I ever had," he told me. Went back to lawyering for the Legal Aid Society, defending the indigent, many of them too dumb to succeed at larceny. He took a job as secretary to a judge who needed serious assistance, which gave him the confidence to run for a civil court judgeship. He won and embarked on a long judicial career, winding up a state judge in the Bronx with an office on 151st Street overlooking Yankee Stadium. True to his Brooklyn upbringing, he never passed through its turnstiles, and true to his education, he faithfully served the people of the Bronx and the laws of the state of New York. He loved his wife, Eleanor, Italian food, jazz and blues and classical music, books of history, and he regarded public service as a high calling. A good man and after he retired, he was ever available to talk.

A city that offers friendships with Mr. Plimpton, Ms. Huxtable, and Judge Globerman is a city I can enjoy living in.

I said that cheerfulness is a choice—well, sometimes it's an obligation. Life can be hard, even brutal sometimes. The phone rings. It's a dear friend, sobbing at the other end. *I can't go on like this. I can't do anything right. I work so hard and I am going nowhere. I don't know what to do with myself.* He is in despair. The play got thrown on the junkpile, the guy who was going to direct it said it's hopeless and my friend knows that's the truth. A year is wasted. He apologizes for calling, we haven't seen each other in three years, but I was the only one he could call tonight. He's in Edinburgh. He went there to live with his girlfriend but that's over now. He doesn't know anybody. All he does is write and write and write and it's all for nothing.

It's strange to hear a man cry like this. Clearly he's out of practice, he's missing his middle range, it's a lot of gasps and whimpers and some squealing sounds. I'm not a therapist but you know what to do, you calm him down, tell him he's good and smart and he did the right thing calling you, tell him he needs to take a break, and when he quiets down, you say, "OMG, I just let the most humongous fart, I've got to open the window so it doesn't get into the furniture" and he laughs and that's good. The poor man isn't going to jump into the Firth of Forth, thanks to your imaginary fart. A year later he's back in the States, teaching high school. A friend calls who has just taken her beloved dog to a pet hospice and she knows it's absurd, a pet hospice, but she's in grief and I tell her the joke about the man who walks in the house with his hands full of dog poop and says, "Look what I almost stepped in!" and she laughs. What is a friend for, if not to tell an old joke? Fix yourself a cup of ginger tea and decide who should speak at Flossie's funeral.

I left Minnesota, the scene of my ambition-driven years, and moved to Manhattan where I do not want. I live with the woman I love, on the 12th floor, high above the struggle for prominence and a parking space, and I amuse myself as a writer. It's a good line of work for me because there's no need to take someone to lunch and try to impress them, you just deliver the goods on paper. An amiable portable occupation. I carry a notepad with me and if I wind up sitting in a proctologist's waiting room, I just write. I arrived at two instead of three for my appointment and it's no problem.

MISS EMILY'S ENEMA

A slender Fellow—is the Hose—
That comes—under—my Skirt—
The Feeling—when the Water flows
And the Intruder Hurt.
The Roaring—of a Cataract
The Fog Bank—in the Room
As if an Arctic Glacier—Cracked—
And made—an Awful—Boom.
This Visitor—unwelcome was
And then Withdrew—from Me—
And Afterward—a Pleasant Buzz—
A lovely—Vacancy.

There is no future in light verse: nobody wants it particularly, so it's a pure pleasure for the writer. I happened on this line of work by being incompetent at other things, which led me to what I'm doing right now as you watch. A cheerful occupation, especially at my age, when my career has mostly disappeared. Nothing to prove, so I take pleasure in writing a very unnecessary poem.

If David Powell could cross the country with babies bundled in a wagon and a milk cow tied on behind, then I can figure out how to make a life in New York.

Pennsylvania was too settled and sedate for him, he wanted spaciousness, and he craved the challenge of fording the Missouri at flood tide, and I should be able to get along with the unmidwestern just as he mingled with the Cheyenne and prospectors. Martha Ann went along with it for his sake and I'm here because Jenny loves the city, hiking around town, dropping in at the Met and MoMA, appreciating the eccentrics she sees in the park, returning from her daily six-mile trek exhilarated and who would deny his lover so much delight day after day.

We go to the opera and for less than we'd pay to fly to Des Moines we see Verdi's *Rigoletto* with the jester singing a great baritone role, the assassin a basso who sings the longest lowest note in opera and the audience goes wild, and the jester's daughter Gilda in love with the Duke whom her father hired the assassin to kill sacrifices her life for him. It's a great evening, probably better than a flight to Des Moines would've been.

It's a great city. Some water mains go back to Victorian times but still somehow work, the subway keeps running, the cops turn out on St. Patrick's Day, the fall marathon is huge, the Macy's Thanksgiving parade. A couple days after 9/11 crowds gathered by their buildings all over the city and sang "America" and other patriotic songs. For months after the pandemic hit, New Yorkers remembered at 7 p.m. every night to stand on a balcony or lean out a window and applaud for the hospital workers. On the other hand, they complain about the president coming to town because he ties up traffic for hours.

New York is not my home but I can reside here comfortably if I remember to be cheerful. I come from the land of slow talkers, rural people with a great aptitude for silence, and was brought up not to interrupt and when I sit down with New Yorkers, who talk contrapuntally and centripetally and all at once, I think of intelligent things to say about ten minutes too late when the conversation has gotten off Buddhism and gone to baseball—I was about to say that some Buddhist monks in Tibet are fans of a song I sang on the radio, meanwhile a guy at the end of the table recalls having met the Dalai Lama in New Jersey once, a name-drop that blows my anecdote to bits, and my wife says something about perfection, and the Dalai Lama guy's brother mentions having met Don Larsen, who pitched the perfect game for the Yanks— and I remember a joke Judy Larson told about Ole and Lena celebrating their 25th anniversary (she slaps him and says, "That's for twenty-five years of bad sex" and he slaps her and says, "That's for knowing the difference") but the connection to Don is tenuous, and now a half-hour has passed, I haven't said a word, and my wife says, "Are you okay?"

Yes, I am. In Minnesota, table talk is like church— thoughtful reflections with meditative silences—and in

New York it's more like a trading floor on Wall Street, so I get a reputation as a dimwit, but it doesn't matter. I can always take the train to 42nd and walk in past the stone lions at the Library and up to the reading room and sit among people one-fourth my age who are busy discerning what is true, what is noble and beautiful, the very people I want to associate with. Most of them, I'd guess, are the children or grandchildren of immigrants so there is motivation here, to justify their forebears' enormous sacrifices. I was 20 once myself but not so serious as they appear to be. My motivation is to justify the heroic efforts to prolong my life; each year is a gift, not to be wasted on watching trashy movies. I hope these good children know better than I how to have fun. I imagine they're on their way to do research on the far frontiers of science and I hope maybe they take up ballroom dancing and afterward go out for drinks and tell tasteless jokes.

New York used to think it was the center of the world, but that time is gone. The semiconductor revolution took place elsewhere, not here, and avarice shifted to the left coast, the tabloid celeb scene died because there were way too many of them to keep track of, and now the city is simply a collection of neighborhoods where people walk their dogs and admire the facades and look in store windows and people my age think how much nicer everything is than in the old days when drivers left signs on their dashboards, *No Radio in Car.* And I admire the cheerful authority of New Yorkers. They love to be asked for directions; it gives them pleasure to tell you exactly where to go. At the opera, during intermission I went to the men's room and a tall woman in a long black coat emerged from a stall and walked out. She smiled at me, having done what she needed to do. In Minnesota, this would've been an international incident; in New York, no big deal: the line at the women's room is a block long.

Emerson said, "New York is a sucked orange," but he didn't spend much time here and maybe he bought a bad orange or the traffic and crowds were too much for a Concordian, maybe his lecture on "Self-Reliance" was not well received here. New Yorkers don't talk about it but they rely on each other. I have often seen people fall on the sidewalk and within four seconds five strangers are there, bending over: "Are you all right?" Twice I was the fallen one. As Tennessee Williams said, "I have always depended on the kindness of strangers." New Yorkers may walk fast but they pay attention and they stop to help if somebody crashes. The cheerful man marvels at it, the great aqueducts that bring water from the Catskills, the rumble of the subway, trains going in all directions. I stand in the front of the first car so I can see ahead down the track, the steel beams, racing into the tunnel, the green light of the semaphore, but the real marvel you don't appreciate until it happens to you: if you're in trouble, strangers will come to your side and try to be helpful.

16

A Cold Winter Morn

I miss our old house in St. Paul, the 5BR one that we sold for a whole lot less than what we'd paid, and I miss the roominess and grandeur of it, the three fireplaces and the terrace and screened porch, the enormous living room where a hundred people squeezed in for concerts. It was the last grand old house I'll ever own. I miss our upstairs bathroom steamy warm on a bitter cold morning looking out on the double row of lights on the High Bridge over the Mississippi. I stand, wrapped in a towel, looking out the frosty window and see no flashing blue lights on the bridge, nobody jumped last night, the desperate of St. Paul decided to call a friend who told them to go back to bed and see what today brings. I turn on the shower and out comes a blast of ice water like what you'd feel if you went off the bridge. I jump back and yell a colorful word. My love appears in her pajamas and says, "The thermostat was set at 85. Do we have elderly people coming for breakfast?" I explain that I had found the thermostat set at 62—"Did the European stock market crash during the night? Are we about to go on the dole?"

She feels that the home needn't re-create the uterus whereas I like it to be toasty warm as if a fire were blazing. So we compromise at 65. Marriage is the true test of cheerfulness—to make a good life with your best-informed critic who's seen you at your worst and could cite examples but chooses not to. It pleases me that she looks at my naked body with interest. After three years of pandemic isolation together, she is the helpless object of my adoration. She corrects my factual errors, scolds me for snacking without using a plate, prompts me to be mannerly, and her keen visual memory means she knows where I left my glasses, my keys, where the peanut butter is in the fridge, the name of the lighting director of the radio show (Janis Kaiser) and I am grateful for these helpful cues.

I adjust the knob, which is not like our old knob, which, in one quarter-inch turn, went from Arctic waterfall to fiery brimstone. This knob sets a precise temperature and the shower head can be adjusted to Needle Sharp or Steady Drizzle or Wistful Mist. But I step in gingerly, one foot then the other, recalling men my age who slipped on wet tile and jarred a couple vertebrae and began a long painful journey through chiropractic and homeopathetic and orthopedic surgery and torture at the hands of a PT named Lyle and then holistic humming and the application of sacred palm leaves, meanwhile your spine is like antique china and your days as a CEO SOB are over, Rover, you are a validated invalid due to one little misstep on wet tile.

In other words, life is perilous. Walk carefully and be thankful for every good day because there are no guarantees, you could trip on a wrinkle in the rug and fall and hit your head and be unable to speak in the future tense. You could suffer a stroke so devastating that your great pleasure in life would be watching golf tournaments on TV.

So I ease myself under the warm shower. Here in the sacred sweat lodge of the Anglo people, a man can't help but be cheerful and I am. I feel some guilt for the carbon fuel used to heat the water to make me cheerful, but not so guilty that I turn the knob to Lukewarm. The hot water relaxes the muscles and also the sphincter trained since childhood—*Don't pee in the bathtub*—and the bladder opens and I feel the pure creaturely pleasure of urinating in a waterfall. My love said to me once, "You don't do that, do you?" I said, "No, of course not." And of course I do. What sort of man steps out of the shower to take a leak? The sort who lowers his voice when saying a bad word. Who says grace when his minister comes to dinner and never otherwise.

I shave and dress and go to the kitchen and make coffee. I look at the paper but there's nothing important. A story about men who feel violated by circumcision even though it was many years ago. A column by a woman fascinated by the infantile degeneracy of men that leads them to want to look at women's breasts. Negotiations continue, prospects of settlement remain uncertain, Democrats are in disarray, church attendance is down again, the obituaries are for strangers. I head to church.

I walk carefully on the icy sidewalk. My brother Philip slipped on the ice while skating, banged his head hard, his brain stem bled, and he died. He was an engineer, a cheerful field of rational problem-solving; he went out on boats on the Great Lakes and studied thermal pollution and shoreline erosion.

His death was a horrible loss. I was in Rome and got the phone call to come home. Sometimes I imagine him explaining his fall to me: "My mistake was that I felt my feet slipping and instead of sitting down on the ice, which I knew I should do, I stood up straight, which meant I had farther to fall, and I fell backward and took the impact on the back of my skull. Shoulder, no problem. Same with rear end or outstretched arm. But the brain tissue is fragile. I was conscious for a day or so but

I knew I was a goner because I couldn't do simple math. It was a big mistake but I'm glad it was my mistake and not someone else's." I want to ask him what death is like, but now I've arrived at church and I go in.

I listen to the Scripture readings, chant the psalm, join the prayers, recite the creed, and I confess my sins.

I say the prayer of contrition
Confess my pernicious condition,
And then in an inst-
Ant am cleansed, at least rinsed,
A sinner but a revised edition.

I have made some persons furious at me, probably for good reason; I didn't take my children camping or read *Winnie the Pooh* aloud to them. I didn't arrange for them to take piano. Mothers do the hard work; Father's Day is ridiculous, a Sunday in June in honor of ejaculation. On the other hand, I've never asked a lover to kill my spouse as Clytemnestra did after she shacked up with Aegisthus after her Agamemnon sailed off to the Trojan War: the two of them hacked him to pieces with an axe, so her son Orestes came and murdered the both of them, meanwhile Electra had gone batshit crazy—this sort of thing has never happened in my family. We didn't even consider it an option. Our nuttiness was of a spiritual nature; we practiced aloofness to avoid infectious false doctrine. I was thrilled the first time I made love to a Catholic. Heresy and adultery in one lovely package.

I pray for those who have sinned against me, all three of them, and for George who was an atheist but switched to agnosticism because his granddaughter is schizophrenic and living in a nightmare and an agnostic can pray whereas an atheist shouldn't, it would violate his unbelief.

I pray for the man I met long ago at Mayo. I drove down there in a snowstorm to find out why I was having so many bad headaches and down around the Cannon River I almost came crosswise with a semi but escaped narrowly. Had I been killed, I wouldn't have gotten the good news that I didn't have a brain tumor.

I sat in the cafeteria, eating a bowl of chili, and a couple sat across from me, a man eating a ham sandwich, his right arm lay limp and useless on the table. His wife looked as if she'd been hit by bad news and was trying to think of something inspirational. And then she recognized me. They listened to my show on the radio, she said. She brightened up. The man didn't. He wasn't interested in making friends. "I hope *you* had a good report," she said. Her husband grimaced. "You've got to look on the bright side. Jimmy and I had forty-six good years together. And doctors don't know everything." I felt bad for her husband. You get old and junk happens to you and you feel the chill in your brain and then you have to put up with all the *God. Damn. Encouragement.* People telling you that each day is a gift. The problem is: you know they're right. He probably thought: "Great. Just what I need. They give me a death sentence and ten minutes later I run into an asshole *author.* And now here I am in his stupid book. If he says one word about maintaining a positive outlook, I'm going to lose my lunch. Piss on him. I hope he gets some utterly new form of impotence and they name it for him."

The church was full that Sunday morning and the choir sang, "We shall walk through the valley in peace. We shall meet our loved ones there." And then a jazzy "Amazing Grace" with Hammond organ, and "I Am the Bread of Life" with Anglicans so moved they were raising their arms up high like Pentecostals. I got choked up and couldn't sing, and then the recessional hymn, "Lift Every Voice and Sing," with people clapping along and Mother Julie dancing like a cheerleader in the aisle, and I walked home, happy having wept, a rare event for me, tears running down my face, I don't do it at movies or funerals, only at church. I composed a limerick. *Our organist Philip Brunelle can make the mighty pipes swell with a stately hymn, proper and prim, or "Ein Feste Burg," what the hell.*

17

Ten Suggestions

Gloom and dread can strike at any time just like when you look up into the beautiful blue sky and an eagle overhead may have an intestinal spasm and suddenly you have something in your eye that you hope isn't what you think it is but of course it is. When life craps on you, you need to get up and move. To get out of the way and also for exercise and distraction. Jump up and down, reach for the ceiling, dance. My wife tells me this and she is right. As I write this, I'm walking at a brisk pace around the Central Park Reservoir, my laptop on a little wooden shelf that hangs from a strap around my neck and my thesaurus in a backpack, which is not true of course but fiction is part of my job description, and work is also crucial to cheerfulness.

1. It's nice to dream, but the urge to write poetry is not in itself an indication of talent. If you can't stop yourself, write a poem and then burn it. If you can't remember it two hours later, this indicates something. Poems usually lead to dark places—drugs, booze, where you don't need to go, so don't go there. Instead of poetizing, be useful: be hospitable to strangers. You have been a stranger yourself and know what it's like. It's awkward. Compliment a stranger on something. Say, "I really like your shoes." Or if they're barefoot, "Where do you get your hair cut?" If they say, "I cut it myself," compliment them on their choice of cologne. If they say, "I just got off work at the turkey plant and need a shower," say "Thank you for your service." Look for the bright side.

2. When the blues lands on you—(is "blues" singular or plural? I say, singular, so it lands, but maybe your blues are plural but how would I know that?)—anyway, it helps to go for a walk along a rugged seacoast where the waves come pounding down on the rocks and be thankful you're not in a small homemade kayak about to be smashed and your body eaten by turtles. If no rugged seacoast is available, you can still calm down by reminding yourself that you didn't stick your head in the oven

or sit in a closed garage with the motor running and a potato in the tailpipe. You didn't eat toilet bowl cleanser. Three wise decisions in one day and they're likely to lead to others. Precedents have been set. Keep going. Having decided to live, why not enjoy it?

3. Don't be drawn into a discussion of feelings, which so often turns into a fetid swamp and people get mournful and self-accusatory. There's a lot to be said for silence; so many situations are only complicated by frankness. You can demonstrate feelings, especially fondness and kindness, but avoid self-analysis and searching for the source. Stories are okay, especially if they're funny. I know a couple who went through a rough spell, got counseling, worked things out, and several years later, they were reminiscing about it—reminiscing about how their marriage was saved—and suddenly everything fell apart. One minute they were congratulating themselves and then the knives came out. The husband spent the night in the guest room and the next night in a Holiday Inn. Put thoughts of disaster on the shelf. The subject of aging is off the table. Brag on yourself a little—recall your latest good deed—mention me if you like. Say, "I ran into Garrison Keillor in the hardware store and he

was buying rat poison. You remember him? On the radio? I asked what it was for and he said he was going to drink it. He said, 'I'm writing a book about cheerfulness and it's depressing the hell out of me.' He had a copy of the manuscript there and he was also buying kerosene to burn it up. I read it while he went to the cashier and I told him, 'What you need is a practical How-To section. Ten suggestions or something.' And he brightened up and got a refund on the poison and the kerosene and the book came out and he never sent me a copy. Said he would and he didn't. Memory loss. He's eighty, you know."

4. Love your enemies, miserable misfits though they be. Shame them with kindness. Cut their throats with courtesy. Place a friendly hand on their shoulder. When they flinch and look to see if there's a knife in your other hand, the alarm in their eyes will cheer you right up. If they beg your forgiveness, look surprised and say, "For what?" as if it's so trivial you've forgotten. "Oh, you mean that time you threw me off the bridge onto the tracks in front of the speeding locomotive? That was exciting. I jumped clear and somehow it cleared up my back problems and I've had no migraines ever since."

5. Accomplish something you've been putting off doing and shaming yourself for. Just do it. Write the letter you owe to someone and have been accusing yourself of indolence and hardness of heart. Put your old tuxedos and wand and cape into a bag and take it to Goodwill: your career as Mister Magic is over. Likewise the three trunks full of videotapes of Bishop Sheen's *Life Is Worth Living* telecasts—the tapes are crumbling and it's all on YouTube anyway. Throw them away. The way to do it is to do it. You'll feel better when it's done.

6. Don't waste time. Time wastage leads to depression. Put a big dish by the door, next to an electric outlet. Put your keys in it, your billfold, glasses, plug your mobile phone into the outlet to recharge. In the time you save not looking for these things every day, you'll be able to read *War and Peace*, listen to Bach's *Mass in B minor*, bake a cherry pie, learn to dance the tango, and whatever else you need in order to be a better person.

7. Most tragedy is misunderstood comedy. God is a great humorist who is working with a sleepy and distracted audience. Lighten up. Whatever you must do, do it wholeheartedly, even gladly. As you get older, you'll learn how to fake this.

8. One secret of the Good Life is to identify your mistakes and try to correct them and when that fails, turn them into endearing idiosyncrasies. I have become well-known for my tendency to misplace things and forget the time and for general ineptitude, which gives the people around me the chance to take charge and demonstrate competence and discipline. Life is not a contest; there is merit in subordination.

9. Music can cheer you up and when you find something that works for you, it may improve with repetition until it acts like a drug. For me, it's Ray Charles's "Smack Dab in the Middle" or the Chopin étude "Tristesse" or Leo Kottke playing 12-string or the Golden Gate Jubilee Quartet of the '30s and '40s. There are other great Black gospel quartets but Golden Gate is crazy wonderful with the booming bass and two tenors and a baritone who sometimes sang falsetto and they bring blues and swing into gospel in syncopated a cappella style in "Joshua Fit the Battle of Jericho" or "Shadrach, Meshach, and Abednego," which leaves you no choice but to be delighted. Back then maybe they fit a stereotype of the Happy Negro but now you can appreciate that they're just phenomenally good. I hang onto my CD player just so I can hear them.

10. And in a pinch, you can sing to yourself. I like
to sing: *Nobody knows the trouble I've seen, nobody
knows but I do.* Sometimes that's enough. Or
there's—
The blind man stood in the road and cried.
The blind man stood in the road and cried,
Crying, "O Lord, don't turn your back on me,
Show me the way to go home.

Which sums up the situation very nicely. We are all
susceptible to mortality. No one is exempt from the
unforeseen. Blessed are the grateful. And vice versa.

Trouble and grief and blindness are all authentic
experience and there is so much pretense and plastica-
ciousness in the world that the authentic is a wonder
like the little kid bawling in the airport, he isn't abandoned, his mom is there, glaring at him, but you hear
genuine feeling in his voice, compared to which all the
conversations in the gate area are the twittering of birds.
My Uncle Lew was the real deal, telling a tale handed
down by his antecedents, an epic of human restlessness,
from a British warship to the Colorado gold rush with a
transcendental impetus from the great Emerson. David
Powell was an extraordinary gent, a farmer who dreaded
the routine and conventional and longed for the road.
The East was settled so he went west. It's magnificent

country and he was eager to trade the rows of corn for the mountains of Colorado. Who could blame him for wanting to see it? He was okay with his failure to find gold—it was experience he craved, life itself.

Ralph is authentic and the words ring. If you go to college and become accustomed to tweedy abstracted denatured discourse about optimization and monetization and branding and molecular ideology, Ralph will come at you like a wheelbarrow of bricks. *All life is an experiment. The more experiments you make the better. Be an opener of doors. Whatever you do, you need courage. The world belongs to the energetic. Whatever course you decide upon, there is always someone to tell you that you are wrong. But the world makes way for the man who knows where he is going. And things refuse to be mismanaged for long.* This man made his living going town to town preaching independence and progress and the deliberate style. He lectured at colleges but also at town halls to clerks and farmers and young men looking for a way out of Weymouth, and there it is: Experiment. Take courage. Make your way.

My Plymouth Brethren were idealists who broke from the Church of England in the early 19th century, back when men were hanged for stealing spoons, aboriginal people were enslaved, the poor were starved into submission, a hereditary aristocracy maintained their privileges, and the Established Church sanctified it all.

The Brethren abjured politics and power and hierarchy. We are all naked before the Lord—so I grew up sitting through Bible study with postal clerks, farmers, a seed salesman, a dentist, offering their comments on what God is telling us. Brother Martin Luther proclaimed a cheerful message in 1517 when he nailed his theses to the church door at Wittenberg, defying Pope Leo X by announcing that salvation is a gift of God's grace, not available for purchase, a message for which he was outlawed but his message survives whereas Leo is mainly known for his diet of worms. I didn't know about Luther when I got revelated. I was fixated on visions of the End, the guilty boy trembling at the Judgment Seat, an angel reciting my sins—disobedience, outbursts of temper, failure to witness to my classmates, the bad words I'd said—and from a grate under my feet I can smell brimstone and see blazing fires and hear the wails of the damned in eternal torment.

I got away from brimstone when I took up comedy, which there is no business like. Mozart wrote *The Marriage of Figaro* two years before our Constitution was ratified. It is a work in progress but *Figaro* is a work of art and people are still laughing at the jokes, the baritone's lust for the soprano, people hiding behind curtains, the seductive note, the wife plotting revenge, concluding with a sweet chorus along the lines of "Let's forgive each other and all be happy," especially sweet since in 1786 people languished in debtors' prisons and small children worked in factories and people felt lucky to live to be 40. Mozart died at 35 from an infection treated today by antibiotics. All the more important to be cheerful, when life is hopeless.

Me, I took my show around the country and wrote songs for Milwaukee ("Where men still wear hats they look rather sporty in/And children take lessons on the accordion") and Idaho ("People move here from New York and New Joisy/To get away from the frantic, the noisy,/For the simple pleasures of Boise"), not works of art, but pleasing at the time. Each one has a role to play. Bruce Springsteen gave voice to the alienated fugitive male and I spoke for Minneapolis:

Cross the Minneapolis border
To find streets in alphabetical order:
Aldrich, Bryant, Colfax, Dupont,
Emerson, Fremont, Girard,
All the order a man could want
And each house with a well-kept yard.

I took a stab at unbelief and then spent a couple decades in spiritual tourism and finally found a way back toward *God is love, and he who abides in love abides in God, and God in him* and St. Paul's note to the Corinthians, *And now abide faith, hope, love, these three;*

but the greatest of these is love and John quoting the Lord, *As the Father loved me, I also have loved you; abide in my love.* It wasn't a dramatic event like Heracles slaying the dragon and getting the golden apple, it was like deciding to stop kicking the wall with your bare feet.

My life was a series of sunken ships and I went to a nearby church and found a sweet upland meadow, which I owe to the love of my aunts, all two dozen of them. They were Sanctified but they leaned toward the *Love thy neighbor* end and away from the scorpions and the sea of blood. They loved me: Elsie, Jean, Eleanor, Josephine, Ina, Elizabeth, Ruth, especially, and now I try to *Come unto His gates with thanksgiving, and into His courts with praise. For the Lord is gracious; His mercy is everlasting; and His truth endureth from generation to generation.* In other words, lighten up. It isn't about you. It's about mercy.

I go to church to think more freely. I mostly believe or believe that I do. I understand those who don't—the idea that omniscience and omnipotence are contradictory, I get that. I believe God will clear this up when we meet Him. But I am moved by the prayers, the readings of Scripture and sometimes the singing is so joyful it reduces me to rubble. Our organist Brother Cantrell comes from the South and he slips "Just As I Am, Without One Plea" into the liturgy and now and "It Is Well With My Soul," and

I am the resurrection, I am the life.
If you believe in me
Even though you die
You shall live forever.

And we sing *And I will raise you up* and I hear my
aunts and uncles singing in glory *And I will raise you up*
and we harmonize, *And I will raise you up on the last day.*
And I weep and so do people around me. There is an
overflowing of spirit, a great mindfulness in the sanctuary—mindful of George's schizophrenic granddaughter
and the two-year-old boy in Atlanta in chemo for brain
cancer and my aging pals and my anxious lover and the
invisible people I've been talking to for years and all
my duet partners and Vince Giordano and his bass sax,
Katharine and Alex engaged to be married, the surgeon
who sliced me open, the ophthalmologist staring into
my eyes as I stare at his right ear, the birdwatchers staring
up at the owl in the park, my grandson Charlie hiking in
the wilderness, Ellie Dehn of Anoka that night singing
Mozart at the Met, the center fielder leaping at the wall
to snag the ball and then casually toss it underhand so
coolly to the kids in the bleachers, and all these New
Yorkers around me weeping—*weeping! Great God in*
heaven, these people are college graduates, Manhattanites,
many of them humanities majors, schooled in irony, they
know what Deconstruction means, and they are weeping

because the cloud is rolled back as a scroll and the faith is visible among us and it is well with their souls. They have been undeconstructed and reaffirmed.

18

The Unexpected Guest

I love church and I also love work as a curative for what afflicts me. Hercules killed his wife and children after Hera inflicted temporary insanity on him, and Hercules, horrified and ashamed, purified himself by performing heroic labors such as killing the nine-headed hydra and capturing Cerberus, the three-headed dog who guards the gates of Hades, and in this way he regained his health, and so may we, if we apply ourselves to the work we were put here to do. There maybe isn't a lot I can do but do that much and more will present itself. When all is said and done, there is more to be done and that goes without saying. A book goes through so much revision, if you knew how much you might never start writing one, but luckily you have no idea.

I'm a writer who learned storytelling by necessity when I was 16 and necked with Corinne in a pile of leaves and came home late and met my mother at the door and invented a story about a drunken war hero and told it well enough to put her mind at ease, and she didn't call Corinne's parents and get her in trouble. The time in the leaves in the dark down the hill from where Corinne's parents sat watching TV was sacred to me then and even more so now and I protected it by inventing a cover.

My awkward years were my 30s and 40s when I worked all the time and came home to angry women who felt I'd abandoned them, which was true enough. I liked work, it took my mind off my troubles, including the angry women. I wrote a weekly radio show based on the shows I loved as a kid that had all died out thanks to TV and I gave speeches to various and sundry and wrote a couple dozen books and destroyed vast third-growth forests in northern Wisconsin. I inherited my work habits from my dad who loved working on his car, changing the oil, spark plugs, fan belt, carburetor. The garage was his office. Other men came to visit him there, squatted around the car or put their heads under the hood and opined about things, and the radio show was my garage. Women produced it—Margaret Moos, Christine Tschida, Kate Gustafson—but I tinkered with it, which was fun. I don't know about plumbing or electricity or even replacing the ink cartridge in the printer. But now and then I walk out on a stage and I talk without notes for ninety minutes and people listen. Performance: the ultimate escapism.

I went through decades of crazy ambition in my working years—shows, orchestra concerts, readings, book tours, much too much of a good thing, and I was crisscrossing time zones and going from EST to PST to do a show in L.A. and lie awake at 1 and 2 with a plane to catch at 7 so I could make it to a benefit in New York for Rich People Who Wish To Help Poor People Without Meeting Them and I couldn't sleep on planes and I amused myself by writing limericks for friends:

A girl who loves radio, Phoebe,
Has AM and FM and CB,
And plays them proudly,
Constantly, loudly,
At about 55 dB,
And when she was caught
She fired a shot
At the cops with her personal BB,
And when she turned deaf
She shouted the F-
Word that's not found in Mister White, E.B.

But the flame of ambition burns lower as you get old, the show-off urge fades. I found that I was describing a world the audience was no longer familiar with—my riff on the fear of putting your tongue on a pump handle in winter because your tongue would freeze to it and might need to be cut off—it got no reaction—because there is not much future in nostalgia. What people want is action and/or sex. *Moby-Dick* would've sold better if he'd placed a couple female stowaways aboard the *Pequod* and they'd shoved the pegleg up Ahab's ass. People want the same as what Shakespeare's audience wanted—dastardly deeds by dark despicable men, a sword fight or two, and saucy wenches with pert breasts cinched up to display them like fresh fruit on a platter. I don't offer those goods.

"Maybe you should," said the reader. She stood up from under the kitchen table and closed the lid of my laptop. "Frankly, there's not a whole lot going on in this book. It strikes me as sort of languid. I hate languidity. Or luminosity. 'Her face was luminous in the moonlight.' 'The sunflowers were almost incandescent.' 'Her eyes shone as she lit the candles.' That sort of thing."

She came around the table and stood over me. "Literature is about a hell of a lot more than lighting," she said. "This isn't a display window at Tiffany's. This is LIFE. Get with the program."

I didn't want to point it out to her but she had aged a great deal in just a couple hundred pages. She was in her late twenties before and now she looked to be around 78.

"Sixty-eight," she said. "I taught eighth grade English for thirty-five fucking years."

"Please don't talk like that in my book," I said.

"Well, if you'd taught eighth grade as long as I did, you'd talk like that, too. While you were standing in front of admiring crowds, I was trying to beat simple basic grammar into the brains of children who despised me. What you earned weekly was my annual salary. Fine. Good for you. But I'll talk any damn way I want to. Anyway, what do you have against action? Other than the kids in chapter one jumping around and dancing, there hasn't been much. Life is more than a mood, more than atmosphere, and writing that isn't about life is dead. It's as simple as that.

She put a hand on my shoulder. "I don't mean to matronize you, but a book about cheerfulness? My God, look at Afghanistan, Ukraine, look at China, the crazies in Congress, the racism that refuses to go away, the migrant children working in the Minnesota slaughterhouses eviscerating turkeys, the ruling class that calls the tune, the plastic we dump in the ocean, people in Congress calling for secession, the world is falling apart. What the hell are you thinking?"

I told her to go back and read the part about avoiding dread, that despair is defeat, that one should do what one can and do it cheerfully, but not sit and soak in the world's troubles.

"There are people running around with guns in this country and every day somebody goes berserk and shoots up a ballroom, a school, a crowd at a parade. And we read it as we get out the chips and guacamole."

I had been so surprised by her popping up out of nowhere that I hadn't noticed her outfit. A black silk evening gown, low-cut, with a double-barrel derringer stuck in her bosom.

"I came in to create some excitement," she said. She reached for the derringer.

"I'm not putting that in my book," I said.

"It's in your book," she whispered. "Sex and violence. Give the dry-goods clerks a thrill. Turn this little meditation into a murder mystery." She cocked the hammer of the derringer.

"Pretend I pull the trigger, Mister Author is cut down in the middle of a book about cheerfulness. The New York P.D. 'll be looking for a retired lady English teacher, but guess what." She pulled the dress down. Hair on the chest and a skull-and-bones tattoo. A Yale man.

He stuck out his hand. "How ya doin'? I'm Billy Bush. Not the Bushes in Texas, the beer Bushes in St. Louis."

"That's spelled B-u-s-c-h," I said.

"You're not the author anymore," he said. "That's the twist in the book, which, by the way, is titled, not Cheerfulness *but* Mister Two-Shoes Hits the Home Stretch. *The prose style changes the moment you're shot and the detectives who find your body with a big hole where the pig valve used to be realize that the perp is now the narrator and we're done with Emerson and American optimism and we're in a jet plane on the way to New York to knock off Russian oligarchs and from their cellphones I track down Putin's hideaway at a cyber-spa in Siberia and put him to rest and head for a golf course in Crimea where I corner D.J. Trump hiding under the name Dmitri Tiomkin and he confesses his crimes and is led away by U.S. marshals who sneak him through the battalion of Russkies guarding him and I shave his hair off with the little ducktail squiggles and I dress him in coveralls and I*

give him a drug that makes him speak Spanish and that's where the cheerfulness starts. Nifty idea, don't you think?"

"I liked you better as a woman," I said. "Much better."

He laughed. "This is 2023, Gramps. It ain't 1951. Gender is a mystery, a puzzle to be worked out. This isn't geology, we're talking about the human heart."

"Not in this book," I said. I pressed Control *and* F *and he was gone and the teacher returned, looking slightly dazed.*

"Thanks for the visit," I said. "And now if you'll excuse me, I've got to finish this book.

And I hit Delete *and she disappeared.*

I just want my message to get through to you. A person can slip into despair as easily as you trip on a curb and land flat on your face and break your nose—it happens on a daily basis to somebody in your gene pool—and you need to get up and go on your way, grateful you didn't break your neck, and cheerfully do what God put you here to do and not soak in gloom about the enormity of the darkness but—and I'm going to go ahead and say it—brighten the corner where you are. I know it sounds Old School but it works and anyway I'm 80. Once I fell, could hardly walk, took a cab to Mt. Sinai St. Luke's on 114th where the ER was crowded with people in worse shape than I. Three hours later, I was X-rayed and a doctor told me nothing was broken, I was okay to go. She was so kind, I asked her to pronounce her last name and I sat and wrote:

> *The ER doc Elise Levine*
> *Is dealing with chaos just fine;*
> *Your calm expertise*
> *And kindness, Elise,*
> *Bring the Upper West Side some sunshine*
> *In the shadow of St. John Divine.*

She was touched. I thanked her and took a cab home. A simple transaction.

19

The Can Opener

Mr. Emerson (1803–1882) lived in an age of invention and he spoke for it when he advocated nonconformity and original thinking, telling his readers to not shrink from their own insights for fear of ridicule by small minds. He was a small child when the railway engine was conceived, and 26 when Mr. Burt brought forth the typewriter. He surely heard about Mr. Morse's telegraph in 1837 and the discovery of antiseptic and pasteurization and the storage battery. When the pedaled bicycle came along, Emerson was quite middle-aged and perhaps lacked confidence to mount one. He admired young men who did but felt it was beneath him, a prominent author and lecturer, to be seen pedaling the contraption along the streets of Concord, but then maybe it struck him—"So let it be beneath me then" and he saw a bicycle in the grass and climbed on it and after a wobble or two he got his balance and soon found himself flying along at a good clip and he felt *moved* by his mobility, racing along too fast to pay attention to the faces of people watching him, and thanks to speed felt truly free of public opinion and now he found himself at the top of a hill and accelerating and realized he had no idea if there was some sort of braking mechanism and he was going too fast to jump off the thing without breaking his neck, and what a way for a great man to die, riding a child's toy. It was a long hill and he passed a carriage and then another, terrified at the thought of crashing, dying, and now his work, his poetry, his essays, all would be forgotten and he would go down in history as a fool, the philosopher who died due to inability to brake, and in his terror he said a fervent prayer and not a Unitarian-Universalist prayer addressed to the Spirit of Truth or the Great Whatever but addressed to God Himself, God the Father and His Son Jesus Christ, as the bicycle flew along and the road flattened out and Emerson realized that in one minute flat he had become a Baptist, a secret that he divulged to his wife and nobody else. He didn't tell Thoreau, he didn't tell Whitman. But God had saved his life on that downhill journey and he was grateful and every morning for the rest of his life he addressed the Divine and thanked God for His mercy.

I'm sure he approved of the corn planter and sewing

machine and other devices to ease labor and grant people more leisure time to think and enjoy nature and converse and read books. Mr. Bell's telephone was expensive and only for the wealthy and surely Emerson ignored it, as well as Edison's wax cylinder, a primitive gramophone, which appeared in 1877. I imagine him lying in the downstairs bedroom, tended by daughters, and hearing artificial music in the distance, like fingernails on a blackboard, which no doubt hastened his demise. I like to think he looked out his window and saw a gigantic gas balloon floating in the sky, piloted by a man in a basket, pushed by a propeller, and wished he could live long enough to try it out. I think flying would've thrilled him. Perhaps his doctor put a stethoscope to Emerson's chest and let the great man listen to his own heart thumping and the great mind be struck by his own physicality. There is reason to believe he was given a pen with a ball point and loved it and wanted to buy a box of them but it was a prototype, not yet manufactured, and the inventor took it back, a sad day in Emerson's life.

Did I already suggest that he, not Washington, is the true father of our country? Yes, I did. There are 39 Washington counties in America plus Washington parish in Louisiana. That's enough for him. The state of Washington could be renamed Zizi, the nickname of the Lakota chief Crazy Horse, whose given name, Tȟašúŋke Witkó, is too hard for us to pronounce. Our nation's capital should be renamed Emerson. He owned no slaves and his friendship with Thoreau shows he was more open to LGBTQ—Henry, if not G, was certainly Q.

In his journal of 1881, he wrote with a newly designed Faber pencil: "Vegetables and fruits, meats and other comestibles packed in steel cans, were the beauteous utilities that sustained our sailing men and preserved their gay natures against the stern countenance of the rolling sea, but gaining access to the gifts was a puzzle. The design of the container, intended to secure the edibles from rot and decay, defied all instruments except a sledgehammer, which likely destroyed the prize in the process of disclosing it. Men inflamed by hunger employed sharpened knives to secure succor and thereby stabbed themselves in the hand and contracted a disease, the blade having been used to gut fish and shuck oysters, and some hands were lost and replaced by hooks, and many good men turned to piracy and wound up on the gallows. Their mothers grieved for them. But Mr. William Lyman toiled in his workshop to invent a safe and reliable device to open metal containers, and he happened on the idea of a proportionate rolling blade turned by a key and following a circular route. He applied himself to this great invention and eliminated superfluous parts, and one brilliant morning he spontaneously happened on the instrumental allegory that opened the secret, the blending of experience and insights of the mind, and from that morning's emancipation came safe sailing between continents, industrial productivity, and a renewed spirit of invention, such as a miniature railroad designed for amusement, moving at high speed on a closed track, a 'rolling coaster,' which liberates us from gravity and makes us briefly weightless as angels, the true gift of transcendentalism and universality."

That was Emerson's last journal entry before he lapsed into silence, the anticipation of the roller coaster that would enable millions of Americans to experience the wild ride he had on a bicycle that had brought him to acknowledge the grace of God that Universalism had denied. He lay on his deathbed, humming "Jesus, Lover of My Soul" as his daughters bathed his fevered brow and brought ice chips to moisten his lips. They considered his humming to be a sign of delirium but in fact it was the dawn of true faith. He died in a state of wonderment and the daughters pulled the sheet up over his face and took the journal and tore out the pages with the tribute to the invention of the can opener and the vision of the roller coaster and the pages were tucked into a hymnal, which made its way west and wound up in Minneapolis in a Salvation Army store where my mother bought it for a dollar and which I inherited along with her black cane. I found the journal pages and, being an English major, I immediately recognized the initials, "RWE," as Emerson's, and I turned the pages over to the University of Minnesota library, which gave them to the Emerson Society and there is still controversy among scholars about their authenticity, which I am not going to argue here—I have nothing to add to what's already been said.

As Emerson said, "The idea of authenticity is flawed by a certain falseness and yet there is profound truth in the meanest lie."

20

Struck But
Not Stricken

L et's be clear about cheerfulness: it's not the be-all
and over-all, the ultimate or consummate and
uttermost. It's a useful tactic to get your head on
straight and go where you need to go and not wind up
in the swamp. Someday you may be old and pitiful and
you'll need to depend on friends who remember you
when you were more fun to be around. Someday, thanks
to good genes and advancements in medicine, you may
live longer than you intended to and find yourself with
blurry vision, cranky joints, occasional confusion, an
unpredictable digestive tract and rogue colon, and suddenly one day you're having to ask someone nearby to
help you go to the toilet. Unimaginable to you now but

someday a plain reality. If you were previously known as an arrogant SOB, the person nearby might find it convenient to slip around the corner, leaving you to deal with it alone. Think about this when you're tempted to high-hat people and spread malicious gossip and be hip and cool and lord it over the unenlightened—think of what it would be like to be standing alone in an institutional hallway shitting in your pants two minutes after some old pals disappeared around the corner. You said, "Could you please"—and they were gone.

We're only talking about cheerfulness; this is not about the Quality of Life. Not about My Most Unforgettable Experience. Not about Fifteen Fabulous Vacation Destinations. The country is in the midst of a gourmet explosion and beer critics talk about "oak flavors" and "breadiness" and I come across reviews of soda pop: *Floral notes of orange peel sprinkled with cinnamon and nutmeg play off earthy vanilla to give this Coke a big boisterous finish.* There's steel-cut Irish oatmeal for when you're tired of the Quakers, there's enriched bionic toothpaste, toilet paper made from eucalyptus trees. The world is doing its best to lift your spirits. You can ask Siri to sing *Jesus, Lover of My Soul* and she or someone else will. This is the life of royalty, no more, no less. Someday everyone will have an AI friend who knows you backward and forward and will automatically sympathize with your troubles but until then you come down to breakfast mourning for your lost youth and your wife says, "What's the matter? The dog peed on your cinnamon toast?" and you grin. It's a good line. Younger people ask if he peed in your latte but I prefer the cinnamon toast. You spread butter on hot toast and sprinkled it with sugar and cinnamon. I realize this dates me but I am what I am, as Popeye the Sailor Man said. You remember Popeye.

So I woke up this morning and felt unaccountably happy. The ship is still afloat, the heroine sent the tenor packing and stayed with the baritone, and so I look forward to another day. I am frustrated by my 14 passwords and other digital mysteries but am satisfied with my lot in life and when I look at the form of my beloved asleep, the fan turning on her bedside table, her earbuds in and a BBC newscaster talking about characteristic colors in newly discovered Phoenician frescoes, the comforter pulled up over her face, I feel a miraculous cheerfulness. Today I shall do what is put before me to do and put yesterday behind just as William Cox did when he jumped ship in Charleston. He could imagine the noose tightened around his neck so he kept his head down and moved swiftly on light feet toward his new life and made it to Pennsylvania and met Miss Boggs and married her, surely a joyful union for him considering the alternative, strangulation, and they produced a string of descendants that includes me. At the time the U.S. population was less than 20 million and now it's more than 330, but certain principles remain, such as doing what you can to make tomorrow better than yesterday.

Life is so full of good things, a plethora, a myriad,
That even if there's an intermediate rough period
Of disappointment and dreariness,
Choose to maintain cheeriness.
Don't let precipitation make you forlorn.
It's good for the corn,
It replenishes the reservoir,
And washes your car
And shows you who your true friends are.
They're wet, their hair is damp, they're none too attractive
But it's a basic fact of
Life, when glamor is swept away by heavy rains,
True friendship is what remains.

I live in New York because my love is a New Yorker and because my eyesight forbids me to drive and Minnesota is not friendly to pedestrians, but I have a flock of friends back home who, when I ring them up on the phone, we fall instantly into warm Minnesota conversation. They don't get worked up about things, back problems, migraines, marital upsets, cranky children, financial reverses, disappointing vacations, and make it a point not to talk about it. "We went to Fort Lauderdale for a week and we were glad to get home," they say. They know we can get snow as late as early June so you shouldn't set your tomato plants out too early. They are loath to speak ill of anyone and if they do, they follow it by saying, "But what do I know?" Their righteousness is muted. *What's the deal with that?* they say. *Oh, for crying out loud. Good heavens.* I can hear my mother's voice, saying, *My, what a vivid imagination you have.* Who's giving you the big ideas? Pride goeth before a fall. The best-laid plans, etc. Man proposes and God disposes. Mother lay awake many a night, worrying about us six kids, she told me so when she was old and we'd gone away. Then added, "But you were worth it." That "you" was plural. She got old and the light dimmed and her back ached, the reward for hard labor, but she chose not to discuss it.

Life is perilous. The race is not to the swift nor bread to the wise. The swift often go swiftly in the wrong direction. The brilliant mathematician goes running and while he does he solves a great math problem in his head and doesn't notice the Wonder Bread truck as it turns right and it mows him down on the street and he dies under a couple tons of bread he never ate. We're not so different from the mouse who scurries through the underbrush only to feel the claws around his neck and hear enormous wings flap and suddenly he's fifty feet in the air being delivered to the eagle's kiddos.

And so what? Sew buttons on your underwear. I plan to maintain cheerfulness at all costs. I keep in close touch with older octogenarians, my advance party, like the band of Crow scouts Custer employed at the Little Big Horn who knew the territory, and my scouts give me a clue about what's to come. My cousin Stan is 90 and has all his marbles so I have reason to hope to remain marbled, which makes me cheerful. Calvin Trillin is 87 and an excellent lunch companion with a good appetite and we reminisce about olden times at *The New Yorker* as men our age should do. And cheerfulness is the key to the kingdom.

When a man has lived a long life, history starts to bunch up, chronology falls apart, I forget what I'm supposed to do Tuesday but remember the names of grade school classmates at Benson School and though I am at the Biltmore Hotel in Coral Gables, I remember how, at recess, we laced up our skates and went round and round counterclockwise on the playground rink except a couple boys who went clockwise just for aggravation. I went with the flow. "Are you happy?" my wife asks. We're sitting under an umbrella, eating lunch, our daughter is executing her butterfly stroke in the pool. I nod. "What are you thinking about?" she says. "Everything," I say. It's true. I'm in love with her and I'm proud of my daughter and I hate the music leaking out of speakers up in the palm trees and I know that an epidemic of stupidity is raging around the beloved country and we see people in positions of power who defy credibility but I also know that an eagle is circling high above to whom I appear to be a mouse and I am grateful for this day and all that may follow.

Sometimes, flying home from New York, the Delta 737 comes over the St. Croix River and I see the Wilcox estate where I lived once and the sandbar where we played volleyball and then St. Paul and Crocus Hill where I lived on a bluff above the Mississippi and where the five EMTs from the St. Paul fire department arrived in five minutes when my daughter had febrile seizures twenty years ago and lay stiff and unconscious on the couch. Four EMTs took charge and one pointed out to me that I didn't have pants on. Never mind what people say, the important thing is who shows up. And the plane circles north and up the Mississippi where I grew up and I can see our toboggan hill and Benson School where we skated. No adult ever set foot on that riverbank, only boys my age, discussing the great questions: What is it like to be 18? And what would you do if communists made you choose between renouncing God and drinking a pitcher of warm spit? And up to Anoka where I was born and where James and Dora farmed and I rode on a horse-drawn hayrack and Uncle Jim handed me the reins, and in from the northwest we descend over the suburban street where my parents bought an acre of cornfield and I watched a bulldozer dig a basement in1947 and my dad poured concrete to make the basement floor and I, five years old, dropped a small iron soldier into the wet concrete, an icon of defense. The shopping mall below used to be truck farms where I picked potatoes and hoed corn. Over Minneapolis we fly, over the lakes, the Dairy Queen on 38th Street where we got Buster Bars before going to gospel meeting at the Grace & Truth Gospel Hall two blocks away, and Bloomington Avenue where I stole money from Mother's change jar to ride a streetcar downtown when I was four years old and was caught in a luncheonette by my dad.

The Mississippi was our reference point. I was born near it, grew up a stone's throw from the river, an independent child slipping away and hiking down a dirt road and along a ravine to a sandy beach under a cottonwood tree where other boys and I discussed Frankie Renko who drowned nearby when his canoe tipped over and where was he now and could he look down and see us. The University was on the river, and the house where my girlfriend and I took off our clothes. And the parking lot where I worked the 6 a.m. shift the winter of 1961. And we are coming in low and suddenly there it is, the hospital where I went when I was 67 and having a stroke.

I was on the phone, talking, and my brain fogged up,

my mouth felt numb, I slurred a word, and I couldn't remember who I was talking to. My head felt as if a balloon were expanding inside it. I climbed into my old Volvo, drove to United Hospital, walked into the ER waiting room, took a number and when it was called, I said in a clear voice, "I believe I am having a stroke." An orderly took me to a curtained alcove and I stripped down to my shorts and put on a hospital gown and lay on the examining table. A neurologist examined me and sent me off for an MRI, fifty minutes of banging and whanging, and I recited to myself "That time of year thou mayst in me behold when yellow leaves, or none, or few, do hang upon those boughs which shake against the cold, bare ruin'd choirs where late the sweet birds sang," the whole sonnet, to make sure it was still in my head. And also "Minnesota, hats off to thee, to your colors true we shall ever be. Firm and strong, united are we." They attached a plastic bag of blood thinner to me that dripped into my system. A neurologist showed me a map of my brain taken by the MRI and pointed to a dark spot: "That's where your stroke hit." And pointed a couple millimeters away: "And if the blood clot had hit there, you would've had significant motor and speech losses. But it landed there, in what we call a 'silent area,' where not much is happening, sort of the Wyoming of the brain, so life goes on as before and you can walk and talk."

Then a speech pathologist and a physical therapist came in. It was comforting to be in the care of extremely capable people who'd aced the math and science courses I'd skipped in favor of the Transcendentalists. My dad distrusted doctors, having a dim view of higher education in general. I don't trust my fellow English majors but admire people who study the data and explain it so an English major can understand. *You suffered a cerebral event that could've been catastrophic. We don't yet know why. We shall endeavor to find out. Meanwhile, we do what we can to protect you against a recurrence.*

I took a walk down the hall of the stroke ward and it was heartbreaking to see people half my age who'd been whacked hard, slumped in wheelchairs or scrabbling along with a walker, and here I was, legs working fine, balance good.

A nurse took my blood pressure, noted my urine flow chart, asked, "How are we doing today?" and I said, "Never better." And I've been saying that ever since.

Someday my turn will come, as I well know. My beloved lumpy gelatinous brain so ambitious to do good things will, in due course, abandon me, and I will sit with a therapist named Meghan who is trying to teach me shapes just like in kindergarten, though I don't have the word "kindergarten" in my accessible vocabulary. O sweet Sarah Bellum, don't leave me to rattle around in a panic of fog, only knowing a vast dimness where the city of memory used to be—I would rather die, Sarah. And you know it's true because, *Duh,* you're my brain.

I asked a doctor if I needed to cut back on caffeine—perhaps change my life entirely, take up running, become slender, virtuous, nimble, pure of heart and deed? He shrugged. He was an M.D., not a doctor of divinity: the stroke was an accident, like a drive-by shooting, and maybe you increase your risk somewhat by living in a rough neighborhood and sitting out on the stoop at two a.m. as the bars are closing, but meanwhile, be glad the bullet hit your left buttock and not your heart.

I came home from the hospital and went back to work.

I did a show at an amphitheater in Wabash, Indiana, with a parking lot full of Trump bumper stickers, people (I imagined) curious to view an actual living Democrat who would take away their guns and tax the pants off them and tell them where they could and could not spit. The crowd sat under a roof and it was raining hard, thunder and distant lightning, and the stage manager and I conferred about whether to do the show and if it were canceled, should the crowd come backstage for shelter. I told them I intended to do the show, no matter what. I stood behind the curtain listening to the storm. The stagehands sat in a row by the bank of rigging ropes. They're accustomed to loading in massive sets and flies, and tonight it's one microphone and a stool. They didn't look happy about being unnecessary, mere spectators. It was still raining when I walked out, rain drumming on the roof, but I walked downstage, which was uncovered, and thought of Prince doing his Super Bowl halftime show in a downpour—he declined the offer of an umbrella and said, "Is there any way you can make it rain harder?"—and (impromptu inspiration) I grabbed the mic and started singing "I'm singin' in the rain, what a glorious feeling, I'm happy again" and the audience picked it up and joined in and then the chorus of "Purple rain … I just want to see you dancing in the purple rain." They were mine from that moment. I owned them outright. I sang a prayer:

Here I am, O Lord, and here is my prayer:
Please be there.
Don't want to ask too much, miracles and such.
Just whisper in the air: please be there.
When I die like other folks,
I don't want to find out You're a hoax.
So I'm not down on my knees asking for world peace
Or that the polar ice cap freeze
And save the polar bear
Or even that the poor be fed
Or angels hover o'er my bed
But I will sure be pissed
If I should have been an atheist.
Dear Lord: please exist.

Then, instead of an *Amen,* I hum a note and they hum along and I sing "My country, 'tis of thee" and they're all there through the dead fathers and proud pilgrims and mountains and I can feel the emotion, they are moved by their own singing, a cappella, me singing a modest bass line, they sound glorious and we go on to the coming of the Lord and the grapes of wrath are stored and the beauty of the lilies across the sea and the hallelujahs—I've given them this chance to be beautiful and they are so very grateful as the chariot swings low and we work on the railroad and we go to the chapel to get married because I really love you and we'll never be lonely anymore, and the audience belongs to me and I to them, we are one, indivisible. The bumper stickers don't matter, we're Americans, the last generation that knows all the words.

And "Going to the Chapel" leads to the story of Julie Christiansen who was 14, a year older than I, and lived in a stucco house that was on my way home from school where I'd been kept after school in punishment for laughing aloud at a limerick about the young man of Madras whose balls were made out of brass and I headed home and there was Julie standing in her front yard. I stopped. She asked why I was kept after school and I told her the limerick. She said, "Do you want to wrestle?" No girl had ever suggested wrestling to me. But it was her idea so I stepped into the yard, intending not to hurt her, and she grabbed hold of me and threw me down and pinned me to the ground and sat on me. It was thrilling. She said, "Let's see you try to get up." I didn't want to get up. And she kissed me, hard, on the lips, and she stuck her tongue into my mouth. I didn't know you could do that sort of thing. Then she let me up. I segued into the pontoon boat story and Kyle lashed to the parasail carrying his grandma's ashes while her boyfriend Raoul on shore held a boombox playing "Love Me Tender" and I thought of William on the dock making a dash for freedom as the speedboat towing Kyle slowed and Kyle lost altitude and crashed into the lake while harnessed to the parasail and was towed underwater at high speed. I had some terrific laughers in the crowd, some cacklers, a lady whooper, a guy who sounded like an old engine turning over, a lady who was a late laugher and whinnied, and they ignited the others and when Kyle flew up naked out of the lake there was general hysteria.

David Powell was an adventurer, a pioneer, tougher and braver than I, and yet here I was in Indiana following in his footsteps, roaming America and bestowing a sort of friendship on strangers, taking a crowd that includes impassioned political enemies and I hum a note and a thousand people sing "O Lord my God, when I in awesome wonder" and they know the words, the stars and the rolling thunder and with all their souls they sing, "How great Thou art" and it is sort of stupendous, and it feels like even the unbelievers got swept up in it and we sing the last line, "How ... great ... Thou ... art" and I put my hand to my heart and thank them. They've given me a new vocation. I'm the only octogenarian stand-up comic who incorporates hymns into the act and it serves a holy purpose: it pulls people into harmony with others they imagined they despised.

Back in my twenties, I was the loner standing outside the lighted house in St. Paul where people mingled and laughed and I envied them and somehow I wound up in radio and gained the power of invisibility and thereby became the host of my own party—what a wonderful life.

A woman at church once told me during coffee hour that she never liked my radio show and we became instant friends on that basis. New Yorkers can be very direct but she said it softly in a friendly way, no toxicity and frankly I'm not a huge fan of myself, so we have something in common. I walked home and a woman walked toward me, saying, "I can't believe you would do a thing like that," and I don't think I know her, and then she passes and I see the tiny cellphone clipped to her ear.

I can't believe I could do what I've done either, but I'm over my regrets, cutting back, living small, seeking simplicity in all things. I despise French cuffs, the search for cufflinks, the folding of the cuff, the complex insertion of the link in four holes They tried to put me in the Broadcasting Hall of Fame but it involved cufflinks so I said no. I prefer a black T-shirt and jeans. I'll keep a suit to wear to church and give away the tuxedos I wore back when I did shows with orchestras so some homeless guy can enjoy looking snazzy. No need for dressing up: in silk and scarlet walk many a harlot. Jeans are good enough and black T, red socks, a pair of comfortable shoes. A belt. Once, carrying groceries out of the store, my jeans slipped down to my knees before I could set the groceries down. A woman whistled at me. I should've said, "Thank you," but at the time I was chagrined. Show business is show business. If you can amuse a stranger, good for you. Too bad my undies were black and not bright red.

If I were more ambitious I'd keep going and write chapter 21 about the advances in civility and social justice brought about over time by musicians and comedians who, unlike the preachers and agitators and organizers, were only out to entertain but when someone you were brought up to look down on makes you happy, makes you dance or bust out laughing despite yourself, it broadens your perspective.

Duke Ellington's band toured the country by bus back in segregation days and if no hotel'd accept them, they slept on the bus. His great trombonist Juan Tizol was rather light-skinned and wore blackface on some gigs so the band wouldn't appear to be integrated. Mostly, Ellington refused to acknowledge bigotry, he just kept playing through it. He packed the Prom Ballroom in St. Paul because the music was great and white people love to dance, same as anyone else. Rhythm is in our system and even bigots can feel a beat, we're a nation of syncopation. You can sit out the dance but still feel moved. He was an ambitious composer but dance tunes paid the bills. He and Fats and Satchmo, Little Richard, the Supremes, Aretha, they changed the landscape.

Mark Twain lost a fortune on the wretched Paige typesetting machine and, bankrupt, had to leave his beautiful house on Farmington Avenue in Hartford and go on the road doing stand-up comedy in England and Ireland and then to Europe. "In Paris they just simply opened their eyes and stared when we spoke to them in French!" he said. "We never did succeed in making those idiots understand their own language." He went around the world, to countries of the British Empire, and he was very funny, even as he grieved for his daughter Susy who died at 24 and he felt guilty about subjecting his wife, Olivia, to the rigors of constant travel and public life, but still the old jokes worked very well.

"To do good is noble. To tell others to do good is even nobler and much less trouble. Good judgment is the result

of experience and experience the result of bad judgment. Don't let your education get in the way of your learning. I was educated once — it took me years to get over it. It's better to keep your mouth shut and appear stupid than open it and remove all doubt. One thing at a time, and just play that thing for all it is worth even if it's only two pair and a jack. Every time I read Pride and Prejudice, *I want to dig Jane Austen up and beat her over the skull with her own shinbone. It seems a great pity that they allowed her to die a natural death. I was sorry to have my name mentioned as one of the great authors, because they have a sad habit of dying off. Chaucer is dead, Spenser is dead, so is Milton, so is Shakespeare, and I'm not feeling so well myself, though the reports of my death are greatly exaggerated. Facts are stubborn things, but statistics are pliable. Clothes make the man. Naked people have little or no influence on society. Always obey your superiors, if you have any. When we remember we are all mad, the mysteries disappear and life stands explained. I've lived through some terrible things in my life, some of which actually happened."*

Twain said that humor comes from sorrow, that there is no comedy in heaven, and his long world tour after Susy's death was a painful time for a stricken man working hard to do his duty and make audiences laugh, but I do believe he took a dark pleasure in it and their laughter was some salve to him, a man with a hole in his heart. In so doing, Twain changed what it meant to be American. After Twain, a sense of humor, a skeptical wit, was required for full citizenship. This is as true today as ever it was. Humor has enabled Americans to survive wars, recessions, natural disasters, and the national hemorrhoid known as Donald Trump. There is no way a person can possibly consider Trump to be an American. He may be German or Swiss, possibly Russian, may have been born to plantation owners in Kenya, but for a certainty he is not one of ours. We are a humorous people and we elected him as a joke just as boys in the sixth grade elected a dog to be class secretary and luckily we got off cheap with only a few trillions in national debt and a corrupted judiciary and the scorn of the Western World and we were fortunate that his bare behind is not on the $100 bill in place of Franklin's face.

No, humorless men have some influence in society, but it's temporary and people are glad to see them go. The culture wars have been won by artists and humorists, not by censors and autocrats and people who go around correcting other people's grammar.

Ellington and his jazz colleagues of the Twenties created music that you cannot hear and not feel like dancing and Twain proved that comedy can survive change and turmoil and decay. "Naked people have little or no influence in society" is as true today as it was back then, and already I'm disappointed that I didn't write that chapter but I will leave it to the reader to tease the thesis—that noble things have been done by people for their own amusement that reverberate far beyond their time and ours. It is a pleasure to find truth that others aren't aware of especially if you don't beat them over the head with it. Creation is cheerful and if your art involves intense suffering you might want to stop and think it over.

Less is more. I have laid my egg and it is enough for today. I went through some terrible years and now I'm not sure they actually happened. Now I only want to be able to do a few things right. Such as knowing when to stop. Though now, as I see I'm coming to the end, I think of so much more I ought to say, such as *I always tell the truth when the people around me know it already and most of this book is true except a few parts that obviously aren't as you probably already have figured out* and also *There is no need for a book critic to bestow superlatives, the pleasure was entirely in writing it* and also *For my next book I shall keep a journal of the rest of my days and it will be thousands and thousands of pages long, filling the box of a Ford pickup truck and wiping out a great pine forest of northern Wisconsin.* And in conclusion, *You have come to the end and much as you dread the thought, there is no more to be had.* Or, as we like to sing:

It's nice to be a saint or
A landscape painter
But in art the employment isn't steady.
Enjoy your lasagna
Though you get lasagna on ya
And the same is true of spaghetti.
You can dream of love
But when push comes to shove
You may have to go out and chase her.
Even great masters
Are prone to disasters
And even Mozart needed an eraser.
Don't sit in the shade,
Join the parade,
Enjoy the bands and confetti,
Put aside regret,
Jump in, get wet,
You'll never get a life if you wait until you're ready.